Comprehension Skills

Level 5
English

Welcome to ■ SCHOLASTIC studySM■RT !

Comprehension Skills provides opportunities for structured and repeated practice of specific reading skills at age-appropriate levels to help your child develop comprehension skills.

It is often a challenge to help a child develop the different types of reading skills, especially as he encounters an increasing variety of texts. The age-appropriate and engaging texts will encourage your child to read and sift out the important information essential to read specific kinds of texts. As your child progresses through the levels, he will encounter a greater variety of skills and texts while continuing to practice previously learnt skills at a more difficult level to ensure mastery.

Every section targets a specific reading skill and the repeated practice of the skill ensures your child masters the reading skill. There are extension activities that can be done for specific reading skills to encourage your child to delve even deeper into the texts.

How to use this book?

1. Introduce the target reading skill at the beginning of each section to your child.

2. Let your child complete the reading exercises.

3. Reinforce your child's learning with an extension activity at the end of each activity. These activities provide additional practice, and extend your child's learning of the particular reading skill.

Note: To avoid the awkward 'he or she' construction, the pronouns in this book will refer to the male gender.

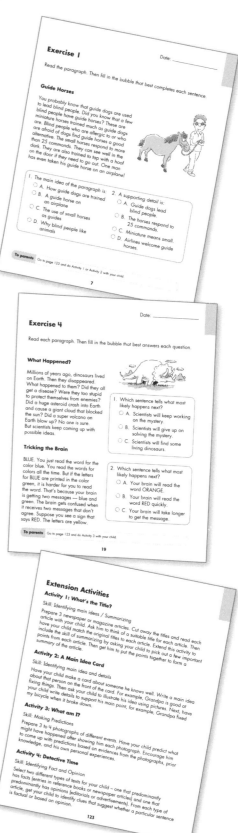

Contents

Identifying Main Ideas and Details

Reading comprehension involves numerous thinking skills. Identifying main ideas and the details that support them is one such skill. A reader who is adept at identifying main ideas makes better sense of a text and increases his comprehension of what is being communicated. The passages and questions in this section will help your child learn to recognize main ideas and the details that develop them.

Understanding the main idea of a passage is to be able to have a broad overall understanding of what a passage is all about. This section will provide opportunities for your child to understand that supporting details fill in information about the main idea and that the main idea is bigger and broader than the supporting details.

The extension activities provide additional challenges to your child to encourage and develop his understanding of the particular comprehension skill.

Exercise 1

Read the paragraph. Then fill in the bubble that best completes each sentence.

Guide Horses

You probably know that guide dogs are used to lead blind people. Did you know that a few blind people have guide horses? These are miniature horses trained much as guide dogs are. Blind people who are allergic to or who are afraid of dogs find guide horses a good alternative. The small horses respond to more than 25 commands. They can see well in the dark. They are also trained to tap with a hoof on the door if they need to go out. One man has even taken his guide horse on an airplane!

1. The main idea of the paragraph is:
   - ○ A. How guide dogs are trained
   - ○ B. A guide horse on an airplane
   - ⦸ C. The use of small horses as guides
   - ○ D. Why blind people like animals

2. A supporting detail is:
   - ⦸ A. Guide dogs lead blind people.
   - ○ B. The horses respond to 25 commands.
   - ○ C. Miniature means small.
   - ○ D. Airlines welcome guide horses.

To parents Go to page 123 and do Activity 1 or Activity 2 with your child.

7

Exercise 2

Read the paragraph. Then fill in the bubble that best completes each sentence.

Festivals in Ancient Egypt

People in ancient Egypt celebrated many different kinds of festivals. For example, there were festivals when the Nile River flooded, making the river banks fertile for farming. Other festivals were celebrated at the beginning of spring and at harvest time. At the celebrations, families enjoyed foods such as watermelons, grapes and figs that were sold at stalls. People also listened to musicians and watched entertainers such as acrobats.

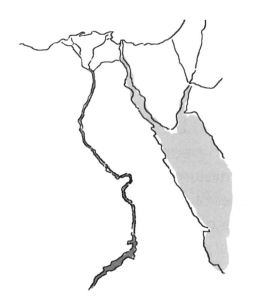

1. The main idea of the paragraph is:
   - ○ A. Why the Nile was important to Egypt
   - ○ B. Watermelons were sold at food stalls.
   - ◑ C. Ancient Egypt had many festivals.
   - ○ D. The festivals honored nature.

2. A supporting detail is:
   - ○ A. Egyptians honored their ancestors.
   - ◑ B. All Egypt's festivals honored nature.
   - ○ C. The Feast of Opet lasted a month.
   - ○ D. People were entertained at the festivals.

To parents   Go to page 123 and do Activity 1 or Activity 2 with your child.

Exercise 3

Read the paragraph. Then fill in the bubble that best completes each sentence.

Jingle Dresses

A jingle dress is for special occasions among the Ojibwa people. Often, Ojibwa women and girls wear a jingle dress at powwows. These are social gatherings where people do traditional dances and have fun. A jingle dress has small metal cones hanging from it like a fringe. The dress makes a jingling sound when a girl dances. According to a story, a jingle dress helped to cure a young girl. That is why the Ojibwa believe that the jingle dress is a healing garment.

1. The main idea of the paragraph is:
   - ○ A. The dress makes a jingling sound.
   - ○ B. People get cured from jingle dresses.
   - ○ C. A jingle dress is for special Ojibwa events.
   - ○ D. A powwow is a social gathering.

2. A supporting detail is:
   - ○ A. The dress has a fringe of metal cones.
   - ○ B. The Ojibwa are from the Great Lakes.
   - ○ C. People camp out at powwows.
   - ○ D. The Ojibwa wear jingle dresses.

To parents   Go to page 123 and do Activity 1 or Activity 2 with your child.

Exercise 4

Read the paragraph. Then fill in the bubble that best completes each sentence.

Eat Your Breakfast

Do you eat breakfast every day? Researchers have found that people who eat a balanced breakfast are likely to be healthier than those who don't. One reason is that most people eat whole grains at breakfast, and these promote good health. Breakfast eaters also tend to have fewer weight problems than those who skip the meal. People who don't eat breakfast usually eat too much later in the day. Often, these foods are not healthy and cause weight gain and other problems. So be sure to eat breakfast. It is the most important meal of the day.

1. The main idea of the paragraph is:
   - ○ A. Breakfast is the most important meal of the day.
   - ○ B. Breakfast is a delicious meal.
   - ○ C. Skipping breakfast makes you hungry.
   - ○ D. Breakfast eaters have fewer weight problems.

2. A supporting detail is:
   - ○ A. People eat too much at lunch.
   - ○ B. No one has time to eat breakfast.
   - ○ C. Only healthy people eat breakfast.
   - ○ D. Whole grains at breakfast promote health.

To parents   Go to page 123 and do Activity 1 or Activity 2 with your child.

Date: _____

Exercise 5

Read the paragraph. Then fill in the bubble that best completes each sentence.

Shoe Making

Long ago, shoes were made entirely by hand. The hardest step was connecting the upper part of a shoe to the innersole. A worker had to stretch the leather over a wooden form called a *last*. Jan Matzeliger changed all that in the 1880s. He invented a lasting machine to do this difficult work. Matzeliger's machine meant that many more shoes could be made in a day than before and for less money. The price of shoes came down, and more people could afford them.

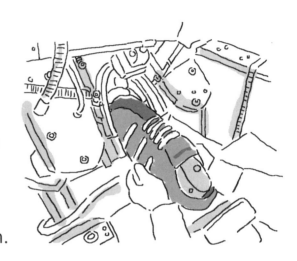

1. The main idea of the paragraph is:
   - ○ A. Long ago, shoes were made by hand.
   - ○ B. Jan Matzeliger was an inventor.
   - ○ C. Matzeliger changed how shoes are made.
   - ○ D. More people could now afford shoes.

2. A supporting detail is:
   - ○ A. What Matzeliger's machine looked like
   - ○ B. Lasting is a difficult step in shoemaking.
   - ○ C. Some people went barefoot.
   - ○ D. The 1880s were a time of change.

To parents Go to page 123 and do Activity 1 or Activity 2 with your child.

11

Exercise 6

Read the paragraph. Then fill in the bubble that best completes each sentence.

Lions

Lions live together in social groups called prides. Most of the lions in a pride are females and their cubs. The lionesses share the work of hunting and raising the cubs. By hunting in a pack, lions can take down animals far larger than themselves. Much of the food killed by a pride is taken by the males. In return, they provide protection from other males. A pride has well-defined territory, which is marked by the males. When lions in a pride meet, they greet one another by head rubbing, licking and grooming.

1. The main idea of the paragraph is:
   - ○ A. Males eat most of a pride's food.
   - ○ B. Lions live in groups called prides.
   - ○ C. Lions hunt together in a pack.
   - ○ D. Lionesses share the work of a pride.

2. A supporting detail is:
   - ○ A. The males mark a pride's territory.
   - ○ B. Lions hunt in a pack.
   - ○ C. Cubs are helpless when they are born.
   - ○ D. Lions are solitary hunters.

To parents   Go to page 123 and do Activity 1 or Activity 2 with your child.

Exercise 7

Read the paragraph. Then fill in the bubble that best completes each sentence.

The Roller Brigade

A roller brigade glides down a boulevard in Paris. This group of inline skaters is part of the city's police force. Their job is to keep bus lanes free of passenger cars on busy streets. They also pull over drivers who are chatting on mobile phones. The best part of their work is posing for pictures with tourists. The rolleurs wear helmets and knee pads as part of their uniform. Even so, it can be tricky to navigate some streets in Paris, especially those paved with cobblestones.

1. The main idea of the paragraph is:
   - ○ A. Paris has a lot of automobile traffic.
   - ○ B. A rolleur wears a helmet and pads.
   - ○ C. Some police in Paris work on skates.
   - ○ D. Inline skates are not just for fun.

2. A supporting detail is:
   - ○ A. Police departments try new things.
   - ○ B. Tourists visit Paris to see the police.
   - ○ C. Inline police keep bus lands free.
   - ○ D. Cobblestones make driving difficult.

To parents Go to page 123 and do Activity 1 or Activity 2 with your child.

Exercise 8

Read the paragraph. Then fill in the bubble that best completes each sentence.

Eyeglasses

Eyeglasses have an interesting history. Early Greek scientists observed that when filled with water, a glass ball magnified objects held beneath it. The Romans used certain rocks to magnify things and aid their vision. The emperor Nero wore an emerald ring for this purpose. By the twelfth century, the Chinese had invented eyeglasses made with rock crystal lenses. Later, in Europe, eyeglasses became a big fad. If a king wore them, so did everyone else.

1. The main idea of the paragraph is:
   - ○ A. The early history of eyeglasses
   - ○ B. The secret of Nero's emerald ring
   - ○ C. Wearing eyeglasses as fashion
   - ○ D. Vision aids have a rock start.

2. A supporting detail is:
   - ○ A. The story of magnification
   - ○ B. From rocks to fashion statements
   - ○ C. An interesting study of rocks
   - ○ D. The Chinese invented eyeglasses made with rock crystal lenses.

To parents Go to page 123 and do Activity 1 or Activity 2 with your child.

Making Predictions

Making predictions is one of the many essential reading skills that young readers need to have. A reader who can think ahead to determine what may happen next or how an event may turn out gains a richer understanding of a text. The passages and questions in this section will help your child learn to make reasonable predictions and anticipate probabilities.

This section will provide opportunities for your child to guess what is likely to happen based on information that he already knows as well as the information in the text.

The extension activities provide additional challenges to your child to encourage and develop his understanding of the particular comprehension skill.

Exercise 1

Read each paragraph. Then fill in the bubble that best answers each question.

Mirrors

People keep finding new uses for mirrors. People began looking at themselves in mirrors in ancient Egypt. In the 1870s the U.S. Army sent messages by flashing mirrors. Today California uses almost 2,000 mirrors to make electricity. A huge mirror in France collects enough heat from the sun to melt metal.

1. Which sentence tells what most likely happens next?
   - ○ A. People will give up looking in mirrors.
   - ○ B. Only magicians will continue to use mirrors.
   - ○ C. Mirrors will be used in more new ways.

At the End

The play was in its last act. The actors said their final lines. Then the play was over. It was a good ending. The curtain went down, and the actors came out to take a bow.

2. Which sentence tells what most likely happens next?
   - ○ A. The actors will sit in the audience.
   - ○ B. The audience will clap for the actors.
   - ○ C. The audience will act in the play.

To parents   Go to page 123 and do Activity 3 with your child.

Exercise 2

Read each paragraph. Then fill in the bubble that best answers each question.

Communicating

Once people used the smoke from bonfires to send messages over long distances. People built towers and used flags to send signals too. In the 1800s the telegraph was invented. In 1876 Alexander Graham Bell invented the first telephone. Today millions of people communicate with computers and mobile phones. Staying in touch keeps getting faster and easier.

1. Which sentence tells what most likely happens next?

   ○ A. People will go back to sending messages by bonfires.

   ○ B. New ways of communicating will continue to develop.

   ○ C. People will get tired of so much communication all the time.

Stonework

Stonework lasts forever, right? Wrong. Over time, stone can decay. Frost seeps into stone and causes cracks. Pollution causes problems. So does acid rain. When a tree branch rubs against something made of stone, the stone begins to wear away. Today many fine old stone buildings are in bad shape. People spend a lot of time and money restoring them.

2. Which sentence tells what most likely happens next?

   ○ A. Builders will take down all stone buildings.

   ○ B. People will try to take better care of old stonework.

   ○ C. People will let old stonework fall apart.

To parents   Go to page 123 and do Activity 3 with your child.

Exercise 3

Read each paragraph. Then fill in the bubble that best answers each question.

Old Money

What happens to dollar bills when they get old and need replacing? For many years worn-out bills were shredded and dumped into the ground. It was a huge job. In recent years, old bills have begun to be recycled. U.S. paper money is made with cotton, so it is very strong. One company now makes roof tiles from shredded bills. Another company is trying to make fake fireplace logs.

1. Which sentence tells what most likely happens next?
   - ○ A. Paper money will no longer be replaced.
   - ○ B. Shredded bills will be recycled in more ways.
   - ○ C. People will start spending shredded money.

Meet Irv

Irv enjoys trying new things. He is always willing to taste new foods. He likes knowing how to do the latest dances. Today Irv is trying to learn how to rollerblade. It doesn't bother him when his friends laugh at his wobbly steps. Ooops! Irv just tripped and fell on his face.

2. Which sentence tells what most likely happens next?
   - ○ A. Irv will give up and go home.
   - ○ B. Irv will get up and try again.
   - ○ C. Irv will hide from his friends.

To parents Go to page 123 and do Activity 3 with your child.

Exercise 4

Read each paragraph. Then fill in the bubble that best answers each question.

What Happened?

Millions of years ago, dinosaurs lived on Earth. Then they disappeared. What happened to them? Did they all get a disease? Were they too stupid to protect themselves from enemies? Did a huge asteroid crash into Earth and cause a giant cloud that blocked the sun? Did a super volcano on Earth blow up? No one is sure. But scientists keep coming up with possible ideas.

1. Which sentence tells what most likely happens next?
   - ○ A. Scientists will keep working on the mystery.
   - ○ B. Scientists will give up on solving the mystery.
   - ○ C. Scientists will find some living dinosaurs.

Tricking the Brain

BLUE. You just read the word for the color blue. You read the words for colors all the time. But if the letters for BLUE are printed in the color green, it is harder for you to read the word. That's because your brain is getting two messages — blue and green. The brain gets confused when it receives two messages that don't agree. Suppose you see a sign that says RED. The letters are yellow.

2. Which sentence tells what most likely happens next?
   - ○ A. Your brain will read the word ORANGE.
   - ○ B. Your brain will read the word RED quickly.
   - ○ C. Your brain will take longer to get the message.

To parents Go to page 123 and do Activity 3 with your child.

Exercise 5

Read each paragraph. Then fill in the bubble that best answers each question.

Catalog Houses

In the early 1900s many people bought their houses from a catalog. They chose the model they wanted and filled out an order form. Then the catalog company sent the house parts by train. A truck took the parts from the railroad station to the building site. The company also sent carpenters and other workers to put the house together. It took about two months.

1. Which sentence tells what most likely happens next?
   ○ A. The new owners will move in.
   ○ B. The new owners will sell the house.
   ○ C. The company will buy the house.

The Forgotten Panda

Each morning Gail walks her little sister to school. She holds her hand and makes sure Carol gets to the kindergarten room safely. Today Carol is crying. She is upset because she forgot her panda for show-and-tell. Gail can't get her sister to stop crying.

2. Which sentence tells what most likely happens next?
   ○ A. Gail will leave Carol at the kindergarten.
   ○ B. Gail will leave Carol on the sidewalk crying.
   ○ C. Gail will take Carol home to get the panda.

To parents   Go to page 123 and do Activity 3 with your child.

Exercise 6

Read each paragraph. Then fill in the bubble that best answers each question.

Album Quilts

Long ago many pioneer families moved west. Sometimes their friends gave them a good-bye party. Before the party, people would get together and plan a special quilt. This was called an album quilt. The quilt was a way for the pioneers to remember their friends. A different friend made each block of the quilt. Each block was signed by its maker.

1. Which sentence tells what most likely happens next?
   - ○ A. The quilt-makers will decide to sell the quilt.
   - ○ B. The family will trade the quilt for other supplies.
   - ○ C. The quilt will be given to the family at the party.

Growing Pains

The town of Woodlands was growing. Some parts of the town had growing pains. The place where Reed Street crossed Broad Street was becoming dangerous. As more cars used these roads, there were more accidents. So the town decided to put up a traffic light.

2. Which sentence tells what most likely happens next?
   - ○ A. The number of accidents will go down.
   - ○ B. More people will begin riding bikes.
   - ○ C. The number of accidents will increase.

To parents   Go to page 123 and do Activity 3 with your child.

Exercise 7

Read each paragraph. Then fill in the bubble that best answers each question.

Watch Out for Hailstones

Sometimes raindrops turn into hailstones. This usually happens in the summer. The raindrops get whipped around in cold clouds. They turn into bits of ice. The more the icy rain is tossed around, the bigger the layers of ice get. Hailstones can get as big as tennis balls. And they can do a lot of damage! When farmers see hailstones, they know trouble is coming.

1. Which sentence tells what most likely happens next?
   - ○ A. The hailstones will be used to freeze things.
   - ○ B. The hailstones will destroy the farmers' crops.
   - ○ C. People will play will the hailstones.

Cathy's Pavement Drawing

Cathy loves to draw everywhere and anywhere. She even drew a picture of her cat, Fergie, on the pavement outside her house. She wanted to show the drawing to her parents. She finished the drawing just as it started to rain.

2. Which sentence tells what most likely happens next?
   - ○ A. The drawing will get washed off.
   - ○ B. The drawing will still be there.
   - ○ C. The drawing will change color.

To parents Go to page 123 and do Activity 3 with your child.

Exercise 8

Read each paragraph. Then fill in the bubble that best answers each question.

Honey

Honey has been used since ancient times. It was one of nature's most amazing products. Early man got sugar from honey. Honey was also used originally as medicine, to make a beverage called "mead", and in a mixture with wine and other alcoholic drinks. In Egypt, honey was used to embalm mummies. Today, honey is consumed by many people in the world and are available in many different flavors.

1. Which sentence tells what most likely happens next?
   - ○ A. Bees will make honey in their hives.
   - ○ B. Honey will be used to preserve fruit and make cakes.
   - ○ C. People will continue using honey for medicinal purposes.

A Sweet Accident

Glenn dipped his stumpy finger into the golden syrup. What a sweet, delicious liquid! He looked around the kitchen. There was no one there. Mum had fallen asleep on the sofa. "Just one more try," he told himself. He tried to remove the bottle of honey from the table, but it was too heavy. The bottle came crashing down to the floor.

2. Which sentence tells what most likely happens next?
   - ○ A. Mum will run into the kitchen.
   - ○ B. Mum will call the police.
   - ○ C. Glenn will eat up all the honey.

To parents   Go to page 123 and do Activity 3 with your child.

23

Identifying Fact and Opinion

Being able to identify and distinguish between a fact and an opinion is an important reading comprehension skill, especially as readers start to encounter a variety of texts. A reader who can differentiate between statements of fact and opinion are better able to analyze and assess a text. The passages and questions in this section will help your child learn to identify statements of fact and opinion.

This section will provide opportunities for your child to understand that a fact can be proved to be true, while an opinion is what someone thinks or believes and is a kind of judgment.

The extension activities provide additional challenges to your child to encourage and develop his understanding of the particular comprehension skill.

Date: _____

Exercise 1

Read the paragraph. Then follow the instructions.

Isaac Asimov was the finest American author. He was
born in Russia in 1920 but came to the United States
with his family when he was three. Asimov became
a professor of biochemistry and a writer. Most of his
books were about science fiction. *Fantastic Voyage* was
definitely his best book. Many of Asimov's stories featured
robots and, with another writer, he created the Three
Laws of Robotics. These govern how robots behave in
science fiction.

1. Write *fact* or *opinion* next to each sentence.

   _____ A. Isaac Asimov was the finest American author.

   _____ B. Asimov became a professor of biochemistry and a writer.

   _____ C. Most of his books were about science fiction.

2. Write another fact from the paragraph. _____

   _____

   _____

3. Write another opinion from the paragraph. _____

   _____

   _____

To parents   Go to page 123 and do Activity 4 with your child.

Exercise 2

Read the paragraph. Then follow the instructions.

How lucky we are when snow begins to fall! Something beautiful is coming our way because the geometry of a snowflake is spectacular. Snowflakes form when water vapor condenses into crystals. Although snowflakes are never identical, they all have a six-pointed symmetry in common. However, weather conditions affect the final shape of a snowflake. These conditions include the temperature and the amount of water vapor in the air. Each snowflake is a work of art.

1. Write *fact* or *opinion* next to each sentence.

   _____ A. How lucky we are when snow begins to fall!

   _____ B. Something beautiful is coming our way because the geometry of a snowflake is spectacular.

   _____ C. Although snowflakes are never identical, they all have a six-pointed symmetry in common.

2. Write another fact from the paragraph._____

   _____

   _____

3. Write another opinion from the paragraph._____

   _____

   _____

To parents   Go to page 123 and do Activity 4 with your child.

26

Exercise 3

Read the paragraph. Then follow the instructions.

The first emperor of China must have been strange. He spent much of his life planning for his tomb. It took 700,000 workers 36 years to get it ready. In the tomb were 6,000 life-sized soldiers made from terra-cotta. Each soldier had an individual face, just like the soldiers in the emperor's real army. I think this is bizarre. Also in the tomb were carriages and horses made from bronze. The tomb was a big secret for thousands of years. Then, some farmers found it while digging a well in 1974.

1. Write *fact* or *opinion* next to each sentence.

    _____ A. The first emperor of China must have been strange.

    _____ B. It took 700,000 workers 36 years to get it ready.

    _____ C. Then, some farmers found it while digging a well in 1974.

2. Write another fact from the paragraph._____

    _____

    _____

3. Write another opinion from the paragraph._____

    _____

    _____

To parents Go to page 123 and do Activity 4 with your child.

Exercise 4

Read the paragraph. Then follow the instructions.

Millions of people in Japan write poetry. That is such a great thing! Everyone should write poems. Everyone should be passionate about poetry. Japan has regular radio and television programs about poetry. It also has more than 2,000 poetry magazines and newsletters.
The country's national newspapers carry poetry columns on a daily basis. Books of poetry are best-sellers. I wish they were in other nations.

Loving the idea
Of poetry for people,
I created poems.

1. Write *fact* or *opinion* next to each sentence.

  _____ A. That is such a great thing!

  _____ B. Everyone should write poems.

  _____ C. Books of poetry are best-sellers.

2. Write another fact from the paragraph. _____

  _____

  _____

3. Write another opinion from the paragraph. _____

  _____

  _____

To parents Go to page 123 and do Activity 4 with your child.

Exercise 5

Read the paragraph. Then follow the instructions.

Have you ever noticed that the print in comic strips is in capital letters? I find this really annoying. One reason given is that comic strips are reduced when printed in newspapers. When print is reduced, small letters tend to blob up more than big ones. Another reason is that by using letters that are the same height, an artist can fit them in the space more easily. I think that artists probably find using lowercase letters too much of a challenge. Maybe they don't know which words to capitalize!

> SMALL LETTERS VARY IN HEIGHT.

1. Write *fact* or *opinion* next to each sentence.

    _____ A. I think that artists probably find using lowercase letters too much of a challenge.

    _____ B. When print is reduced, small letters tend to blob up more than big ones.

    _____ C. Maybe they don't know which words to capitalize!

2. Write another fact from the paragraph. _____

    _____

    _____

3. Write another opinion from the paragraph. _____

    _____

    _____

To parents   Go to page 123 and do Activity 4 with your child.

Exercise 6

Read the paragraph. Then follow the instructions.

A huge mountain system stretches across 1,500 miles of Asia. This mountain range is called the Himalayas. The mountains were formed about 60 million years ago. The world's 10 tallest mountains are all in the Himalayas. That's amazing! Mount Everest, which lies between Tibet and Nepal, is the world's highest mountain. It reaches up for 29,028 feet, too high for even birds to fly. The first climbers to reach the top did so in 1953. They must have been brave. Their names were Sir Edmund Hillary and Tenzing Norgay.

1. Write *fact* or *opinion* next to each sentence.

    _____ A. This mountain range is called the Himalayas.

    _____ B. That's amazing!

    _____ C. The first climbers to reach the top did so in 1953.

2. Write another fact from the paragraph._____

    _____

    _____

3. Write another opinion from the paragraph._____

    _____

    _____

To parents   Go to page 123 and do Activity 4 with your child.

Exercise 7

Read the paragraph. Then follow the instructions.

Kids who like to get muddy should visit Westland, Michigan. This city hosts an annual celebration called Mud Day in Hines Park. It must be a sloppy mess. The parks department mixes more than 200 tons of soil and 20,000 gallons of water to make mud. That's a lot of mud! There are events such as a Mud Limbo contest, wheelbarrow races, and just plain splashing around. Two participants are crowned Mr and Miss Mud. When the fun is over, firefighters hose down the dirty kids.

1. Write *fact* or *opinion* next to each sentence.

   _____ A. Kids who like to get muddy should visit Westland, Michigan.

   _____ B. It must be a sloppy mess.

   _____ C. Two participants are crowned Mr and Miss Mud.

2. Write another fact from the paragraph._____

   _____

   _____

3. Write another opinion from the paragraph._____

   _____

   _____

To parents   Go to page 123 and do Activity 4 with your child.

Exercise 8

Read the paragraph. Then follow the instructions.

A large granite head rises out of Thunderhead Mountain in South Dakota. The head is magnificent. It is part of a sculpture called the Crazy Horse Memorial, which is being carved from the mountain. Crazy Horse was a Sioux warrior who defeated Lieutenant Colonel George Armstrong Custer at the Battle of Little Bighorn in 1877. The memorial was begun in 1948 by Korzak Ziolkowski. It's taken much too long to complete. When finished, however, it will be 563 feet tall and 641 feet long.

1. Write *fact* or *opinion* next to each sentence.

   _____ A. A large granite head rises out of Thunderhead Mountain in South Dakota.

   _____ B. The memorial was begun in 1948 by Korzak Ziolkowski.

   _____ C. It's taken much too long to complete.

2. Write another fact from the paragraph._____

   _____

   _____

3. Write another opinion from the paragraph._____

   _____

   _____

To parents   Go to page 123 and do Activity 4 with your child.

Date: _____

Exercise 9

Read the paragraph. Then follow the instructions.

You should thank the Navajos. During World War II,
350 of them worked as code talkers. They sent messages
in the Navajo language for the American military. Both
sides used codes during the war, but most codes can
eventually be broken. You have to be brilliant to break a
code. However, little of the Navajo language had ever been written down. It was
hard to learn, and it was very different from other languages. So although many
radio messages were intercepted, the enemy couldn't break the Navajo code.

1. Write *fact* or *opinion* next to each sentence.

   _____ A. You should thank the Navajos.

   _____ B. They sent messages in the Navajo language for the
   American military.

   _____ C. Both sides used codes during the war, but most codes can
   eventually be broken.

2. Write another fact from the paragraph._____

   _____

   _____

3. Write another opinion from the paragraph._____

   _____

   _____

To parents   Go to page 123 and do Activity 4 with your child.

Exercise 10

Read the paragraph. Then follow the instructions.

Vegetables and fruits of the future may differ from those you eat today. Scientists in China have been sending seeds into space. The seeds are exposed to different extraterrestrial conditions that change the DNA of the seeds. The seeds are then planted back on Earth. The results are disturbing. Some examples are cucumbers the length of baseball bats and monster eggplants. They must taste terrible. These veggies aren't for sale to the public yet. They're probably not safe!

1. Write *fact* or *opinion* next to each sentence.

   _____ A. The results are disturbing.

   _____ B. These veggies aren't for sale to the public yet.

   _____ C. They must taste terrible.

2. Write another fact from the paragraph._____

   _____

   _____

3. Write another opinion from the paragraph._____

   _____

   _____

To parents   Go to page 123 and do Activity 4 with your child.

Comparing and Contrasting

Making comparisons is an essential reading comprehension skill that enriches a reader's understanding of the text. A reader who can compare and contrast events, characters, places, and facts is able to identify similarities and differences, and to categorize or group information. The passages and questions in this section will help your child learn to compare and contrast.

This section will provide opportunities for your child to understand that comparing and contrasting helps him to organize and comprehend information in the text. This is essential especially as your child encounters more non-fiction texts.

The extension activities provide additional challenges to your child to encourage and develop his understanding of the particular comprehension skill.

Date: _____

Exercise 1

Read the paragraph. Then answer the questions.

Yesterday and Today

What was it like to live in a city in ancient Rome? You would find roads paved with stone. There were public gardens for all to enjoy like the parks of today. For water, people went to public fountains. There were also public baths. Today people just turn on the tap in their homes. Roman books were on scrolls. Boys went to school but girls did not. That's not how it is in the U.S. today!

1. How was life in ancient Rome like life today?

   ○ A. People took baths then and today.

   ○ B. Only boys went to school.

   ○ C. People got water from public fountains.

2. How was life in ancient Rome different from life today?

   ○ A. Cities had public parks or gardens.

   ○ B. To wash, the Romans went to a public bath.

   ○ C. Roads were paved then and today.

3. Write another way that life in ancient Rome was different from life today.

   _____

   _____

   _____

   _____

   _____

   _____

To parents Go to page 124 and do Activity 5 with your child.

36

Exercise 2

Read the paragraph. Then answer the questions.

Big Rhinos

Rhinos are big, bulky animals that live in Africa.
Rhinos have poor eyesight but good hearing.
They also have a good sense of smell. Rhinos
are very strong and are feared by enemies. The
white rhino is heavier than the black rhino. Both
kinds are plant-eaters. They chomp on grasses
and bushes. The white rhino has a wide, square
upper lip. The black rhino's upper lip is pointed.
Both kinds of rhinos are endangered.

1. How are the white rhino and the
   black rhino alike?

   ○ A. They are very strong.

   ○ B. They have wide, square
        lips.

   ○ C. They are the same size.

2. How are the white rhino and the
   black rhino different?

   ○ A. The black rhino has a
        pointed lip.

   ○ B. The white rhino eats plants.

   ○ C. The black rhino has poor
        eyesight.

3. Write another way the white rhino
   and the black rhino are alike.

   _____

   _____

   _____

   _____

   _____

   _____

To parents   Go to page 124 and do Activity 5 with your child.

Exercise 3

Read the paragraph. Then answer the questions.

Comparing Camels

Camels are desert animals that live in Africa and Asia. These animals are hard workers. They can go weeks without food or water. The Bactrian camel has two humps. Sometimes this camel spits. People weave its fur into cloth. The dromedary is a camel with one hump. It is sometimes trained for racing. Both kinds of camels groan when they have to rise with heavy loads. They can also kick.

1. How are Bactrian camels and dromedaries alike?

   ○ A. They sometimes spit.

   ○ B. They have one hump.

   ○ C. They are hard workers.

2. How are Bactrian camels and dromedaries different?

   ○ A. Dromedaries can go for weeks without food.

   ○ B. Bactrian camels have two humps.

   ○ C. Dromedaries live in Asia and Africa.

3. Write another way that dromedaries and Bactrian camels are alike.

   _____

   _____

   _____

   _____

   _____

   _____

To parents Go to page 124 and do Activity 5 with your child.

Date: _____

Exercise 4

Read the paragraph. Then answer the questions.

Tale of Two Cities

The two largest cities in Pennsylvania are Philadelphia and Pittsburgh. Philadelphia is in the eastern part of the state. Pittsburgh is in the western part. Philadelphia is on the Delaware River. Pittsburgh is on the Allegheny, Monongahela and Ohio rivers. Founded in 1682, Philadelphia is older. Its nickname is the City of Brotherly Love. Pittsburgh was once the center of the steel industry. It was called Steel City.

1. How are Philadelphia and Pittsburgh alike?

   ○ A. They are in western Pennsylvania.

   ○ B. They were once steel centers.

   ○ C. They are located on rivers.

2. How are Philadelphia and Pittsburgh different?

   ○ A. Pittsburgh is a large city.

   ○ B. Philadelphia is sometimes called by a nickname.

   ○ C. Philadelphia is on the Delaware River.

3. Write another way that Philadelphia and Pittsburgh are different.

   _____

   _____

   _____

   _____

   _____

   _____

To parents   Go to page 124 and do Activity 5 with your child.

Exercise 5

Read the paragraph. Then answer the questions.

Tall-Tale Characters

In the early days of our country, people told tall tales. These were about characters with larger-than-life powers. One was Paul Bunyan, a lumberman. He had a blue ox named Babe. Paul did things in a big way. When he needed drinking water, he dug some ponds. They became the Great Lakes. Pecos Bill was a tall-tale cowboy. He rode a horse named Widow-Maker. He taught broncos how to buck. He also invented scorpions as a joke.

1. How were Paul Bunyan and Pecos Bill alike?

   ○ A. They had larger-than-life powers.

   ○ B. They were mighty lumbermen.

   ○ C. They taught broncos how to buck.

2. How were Paul Bunyan and Pecos Bill different?

   ○ A. Paul was a tall-tale character.

   ○ B. Pecos Bill had a special animal.

   ○ C. Pecos Bill invented scorpions.

3. Write another way that Paul Bunyan and Pecos Bill were different.

   _____

   _____

   _____

   _____

   _____

   _____

To parents   Go to page 124 and do Activity 5 with your child.

Date: _____

Exercise 6

Read the paragraph. Then answer the questions.

All About Bridges

People cross bridges to get from one place to another. The bridges of today are based on ideas from the past. Some bridges rest on posts called piers. These are girder or beam bridges. They are built like early temples that had pillars to hold up the roof. Another kind of bridge is the suspension bridge. It has tall towers. Big steel cables hang from the towers and support the bridge. Early models for these bridges were vine and rope bridges.

1. How were girder and suspension bridges alike?

   ○ A. People use them to get from one place to another.

   ○ B. They were near towers.

   ○ C. They were built like templates.

2. How were girder and suspension bridges different?

   ○ A. They were based on the past.

   ○ B. Early models of suspension bridges were vine and rope bridges.

   ○ C. Suspension bridges rest on pillars.

3. Write another way that girder and suspension bridges are different.

   _____

   _____

   _____

   _____

   _____

   _____

To parents Go to page 124 and do Activity 5 with your child.

Exercise 7

Read the paragraph. Then answer the questions.

Changes Over Time

Many children have pet dogs or cats today. In Egypt about 3,000 years ago, children also had pet cats. They had pet monkeys too. In school a boy of ancient Egypt would write on papyrus. Girls were not allowed to go to school. Today boys and girls attend school and do their writing on paper. Like children today, children in ancient Egypt enjoyed going to parties.

1. How was life in ancient Egypt and life in Egypt today alike?

   ○ A. Girls could not go to school.

   ○ B. Children write on paper.

   ○ C. Children kept pets.

2. How was life in ancient Egypt and life in Egypt today different?

   ○ A. Girls could go to parties.

   ○ B. Boys in ancient Egypt would write on papyrus.

   ○ C. Boys kept pets.

3. Write another way that life in ancient Egypt was different from life today.

   _____

   _____

   _____

   _____

   _____

   _____

To parents Go to page 124 and do Activity 5 with your child.

42

Exercise 8

Read the paragraph. Then answer the questions.

McDonald's and Kentucky Fried Chicken

McDonald's and Kentucky Fried Chicken (KFC) are popular fast food chains in many countries. They both offer food that is affordable to the general public and in a speedy fashion. KFC entered the fast food business about ten years before McDonald's. McDonald's mascot is a smiling clown in bright, yellow costume, while KFC's mascot is the cartoonised version of its original creator. While McDonald's menu is dominated by burgers, KFC's menu is predominantly fried chicken.

1. How are McDonald's and KFC alike?

   ○ A. They have the same mascot.

   ○ B. They both serve affordable food.

   ○ C. They both started business at the same time.

2. How are McDonald's and KFC different?

   ○ A. McDonald's mainly sells burgers.

   ○ B. KFC sells food in a speedy fashion.

   ○ C. McDonald's can be found in many countries.

3. Write another way that McDonald's and KFC are different.

   _____

   _____

   _____

   _____

   _____

To parents   Go to page 124 and do Activity 5 with your child.

Exercise 9

Read the paragraph. Then answer the questions.

From Film to Digital

Cameras are used to take photographs and preserve images.
The first camera to use photographic film was called the Kodak.
Cameras in the past had to be pre-loaded with film. Once the
roll of film was used up, the roll had to be sent back to the shop
for processing. More people these days use digital cameras.
Instead of film, digital cameras capture and save photographs on
digital memory cards and do not need to be sent to a shop to be
processed. The photographs can be easily transferred and shared with others.

1. How are film cameras and digital
   cameras alike?

   ○ A. They both have to be loaded
          with film.

   ○ B. They both use photographic film.

   ○ C. They both take photographs.

2. How are film cameras and digital
   cameras different?

   ○ A. Digital cameras do not use film.

   ○ B. Film cameras take photographs that
          can easily be shared with others.

   ○ C. Digital memory cards and film rolls
          have to be processed at the store.

3. Write another way that film
   cameras and digital cameras
   are different.

   _____

   _____

   _____

   _____

   _____

   _____

To parents   Go to page 124 and do Activity 5 with your child.

44

Exercise 10

Read the paragraph. Then answer the questions.

Tornadoes and Hurricanes

Tornadoes and hurricanes both consist of large columns of air and powerful winds. They are natural phenomenon that can cause a lot of damage and destruction. Unlike tornadoes, hurricanes are often accompanied by heavy rain and flooding. They often form over warm ocean water. Hurricanes tend to last several days while tornadoes last from a few seconds to several minutes. Tornadoes form over land. They cause destruction through wind power and flying debris.

1. How are tornadoes and hurricanes alike?

   ○ A. They both cause flooding.

   ○ B. They both last for a very short period of time.

   ○ C. They both cause a lot of damage.

2. How are tornadoes and hurricanes different?

   ○ A. Tornadoes are man-made.

   ○ B. Hurricanes last longer.

   ○ C. Tornadoes cause more damage.

3. Write another way that tornadoes and hurricanes are different.

   _____

   _____

   _____

   _____

   _____

   _____

To parents Go to page 124 and do Activity 5 with your child.

Using Context Clues

Being able to use context clues to make accurate estimations of unfamiliar words or phrases is essential in helping a reader better understand what is being communicated in a text. Very often, writers may use words that are unfamiliar to readers. However, there are often clues in the rest of the text to point to what that word means. Readers need to be able to sift out those clues to make sense of the text. The passages and questions in this section will help your child learn to use contextual clues to understand difficult or unfamiliar vocabulary.

This section will provide opportunities for your child to understand that using contextual clues means to look at the rest of the passage to try and figure out what a particular word or phrase means. This is especially the case when the writer does not explicitly provide the definition of the word in the passage because that would interrupt the flow of the passage. This is important as your child encounters a variety of texts and writing styles.

The extension activities provide additional challenges to your child to encourage and develop his understanding of the particular comprehension skill.

Date: _____

Exercise 1

Read each paragraph. Then fill in the bubble that best completes each sentence.

Cook's Trip

In 1770 Captain James Cook was sailing in the Pacific Ocean. He was on his way home to England. A bad storm came up. Cook's ship was blown toward some land. He sailed along the shore. On the land he saw many new plants and animals. Captain Cook decided to **claim** the land for England. The land was known as Australia. England ruled it for many years.

1. In this paragraph, the word **claim** must mean
   ○ A. make a map of
   ○ B. make a sudden sound
   ○ C. state the right to own

Bret and Brad

The twins were alike in many ways. But when it came to swimming, they had different ideas. Bret liked to get into the water slowly. Sometimes he took quite a long time. But Brad liked to get in fast. He would **plunge** right in and come up laughing. Bret could never understand this.

2. In this paragraph, the word **plunge** must mean
   ○ A. play fairly
   ○ B. enter quickly
   ○ C. throw down

To parents   Go to page 124 and do Activity 8 with your child.

Exercise 2

Read each paragraph. Then fill in the bubble that best completes each sentence.

In the U.S.

Parts of the United States are rolling meadows called **prairies**. These regions have deep, rich soil. The land is mostly flat. Prairies do not get enough rain for many trees to grow. But grasses grow well on them. These areas are good for growing grains such as wheat and oats. The prairies are also good for raising animals that eat grass, such as cattle.

1. In this paragraph, the word **prairies** must mean
   - ○ A. drylands
   - ○ B. wetlands
   - ○ C. grasslands

Abby's Talk

Abby was asked to give a talk in school. She was **eager** to do this. Abby liked to talk. She was good at getting people to listen. She could make people laugh, too. When the time for her talk came, Abby was ready. She gave a great talk.

2. In this paragraph, the word **eager** must mean
   - ○ A. wanting to do something
   - ○ B. unhappy about being chosen
   - ○ C. not interested in a project

To parents   Go to page 124 and do Activity 8 with your child.

Exercise 3

Read each paragraph. Then fill in the bubble that best completes each sentence.

The Ocean Floor

Most people think of the bottom of the ocean as a flat place. But it is not. It is much like the rest of Earth—uneven. In some places the ocean bottom slopes downward from the shore. In other places it is flat. There are also lots of mountains. Between the mountains are deep **trenches**. The Mariana Trench in the Pacific Ocean is almost 40,000 feet deep.

1. In this paragraph, the word **trenches** must mean
   - ○ A. big ditches
   - ○ B. areas where the land trembles
   - ○ C. mountains on the floor of the ocean

Fred the Fish

Fred was a very smart fish. He lived in a peaceful river. Nothing much happened there unless people came around. Then Fred had to be **alert**. A yummy worm might mean a trap. If Fred wasn't careful, he could end up as someone's supper. He had seen it happen to many careless fish.

2. In this paragraph, the word **alert** must mean
   - ○ A. watchful
   - ○ B. careless
   - ○ C. sleepy

To parents   Go to page 124 and do Activity 8 with your child.

Exercise 4

Read each paragraph. Then fill in the bubble that best completes each sentence.

Languages of the World

Not everyone in the world speaks English. In fact, more people speak Chinese than any other language in the world. English is the second-most-spoken language. Other **major** languages are Russian and Hindi. More than 300 million people speak Hindi. Most of these people are from India.

1. In this paragraph, the word **major** must mean
   - ○ A. foreign and unknown
   - ○ B. large and important
   - ○ C. difficult and different

The Race

The race was about to begin. The announcer asked for the crowd's attention. Then he told the runners to take their places at the starting line. For a **brief** moment, there was silence. Then the announcer yelled, "Ready! Set! Go!" The race was on. The runners were off around the track, and the crowd started cheering.

2. In this paragraph, the word **brief** must mean
   - ○ A. rude
   - ○ B. noisy
   - ○ C. short

To parents Go to page 124 and do Activity 8 with your child.

Exercise 5

Read each paragraph. Then fill in the bubble that best completes each sentence.

Rail Trails

What happens to unused railroad tracks? In many parts of the U.S., people take part in a Rails to Trails program. They **convert** the tracks to trails. Smooth paths are laid down where the tracks once ran. People use these rail trails for walking, jogging, skating, and bike riding. In winter the trails are great for cross-country skiing too.

1. In this paragraph, the word **convert** must mean
   ○ A. carry
   ○ B. discuss
   ○ C. change

A Fresh Flower

Don's class was learning about plants. The teacher asked the students to bring in a flower. Don chose a pretty flower from his mother's garden."How will I get this to school?" he asked."The flower will **wilt** on the bus."Don's mother showed him what to. She wrapped a wet paper towel around the flower stem."This will keep your flower alive until you can put it in water,"she said.

2. In this paragraph, the word **wilt** must mean
   ○ A. spill over
   ○ B. lose freshness
   ○ C. grow slowly

To parents   Go to page 124 and do Activity 8 with your child.

Exercise 6

Read each paragraph. Then fill in the bubble that best completes each sentence.

Furniture of the Past

In early America most furniture was made by hand. Many people had only a few pieces in their homes. So furniture such as chairs sometimes had more than one **function**. For example, a ladder-backed chair could be used for sitting. It could also be used as a ladder. A rocking chair also served as a baby's cradle. Some chairs could be used to hold up shelves.

1. In this paragraph, the word **function** must mean
   - ○ A. cushion
   - ○ B. future
   - ○ C. use

The Sandwich

Mr Greenberg made a sandwich for his lunch. As he set it on the table, the doorbell rang. When Mr Greenberg came back, his sandwich was gone. But Mr Greenberg knew what had happened. He had seen his dog **seize** the sandwich and run. Right now Old Pal was sitting on the porch licking his lips.

2. In this paragraph, the word **seize** must mean
   - ○ A. grab
   - ○ B. sniff
   - ○ C. leave

To parents   Go to page 124 and do Activity 8 with your child.

Exercise 7

Read each paragraph. Then fill in the bubble that best completes each sentence.

An Old Custom

A "baker's dozen" is 13 instead of 12. The custom goes back to the year 1266 in England. Bakers were making small loaves of bread. People did not get what they paid for. So laws were passed. The laws said that bakers had to meet **standards** set by the government. To be sure that they met these measures, bakers gave people an extra loaf when they ordered a dozen.

1. In this paragraph, the word **standards** must mean
   ○ A. special stamps for bread
   ○ B. well-known measures
   ○ C. extra pieces of bread

Garbage Day

The bags of garbage were lined up at the curb. Down the street came the truck. At each stop the men got out and picked up the bags. One by one they **heaved** the heavy bags into the back of the truck. As the bags dropped into the truck, they made crashing, clunking sounds.

2. In this paragraph, the word **heaved** must mean
   ○ A. pulled
   ○ B. lifted
   ○ C. opened

To parents   Go to page 124 and do Activity 8 with your child.

Exercise 8

Read each paragraph. Then fill in the bubble that best completes each sentence.

The Mighty Python

Meet the python. This mighty snake grows up to 23 feet long. When the python is hungry, it needs a big meal. A python might grab a wild pig or small deer for dinner. The snake wraps itself around the animal until it is dead. Then the python opens its mouth and its dinner **vanishes** in one large gulp. After that, a python may not need to eat again for a while.

1. In this paragraph, the word **vanishes** must mean
   ○ A. disappears
   ○ B. runs away
   ○ C. stretches

Good Morning, Jade

Jade was always in a hurry. She ran into the kitchen for breakfast. She drank her juice in no time. She quickly dumped cereal into a bowl. Then she rushed to grab the pitcher of milk. "Slow down, Jade," her mother said. But it was too late. The pitcher slipped. Milk **gushed** out onto Jade's cereal and over the table as well. Jade cleaned up the mess. "Did you see how fast that milk came out?" she said.

2. In this paragraph, the word **gushed** must mean
   ○ A. gasped
   ○ B. dripped
   ○ C. poured

To parents Go to page 124 and do Activity 8 with your child.

Exercise 9

Read each paragraph. Then fill in the bubble that best completes each sentence.

Body Temperature

As you climb out of the swimming pool, a breeze blows up. You can't find your towel. You are chilly. You begin to shiver. What makes you shiver? When your body temperature drops, a part of your brain quickly **reacts**. It takes control of your muscles and makes you shiver. When you shiver, you make extra body heat. This helps you warm up.

1. In this paragraph, the word **reacts** must mean
   - ○ A. warms up
   - ○ B. shuts down
   - ○ C. acts in response

A Book Sale

The town was having a used-book sale to raise money. People were asked to **donate** books they no longer wanted. Money from the sale would help to fix up the town park. Cole planned to give three books that were too easy for him. At the sale he hoped to buy other books that he hadn't yet read.

2. In this paragraph, the word **donate** must mean
   - ○ A. read
   - ○ B. dump
   - ○ C. give

To parents   Go to page 124 and do Activity 8 with your child.

Exercise 10

Read each paragraph. Then fill in the bubble that best completes each sentence.

Henson's Medal

Matthew Henson was an explorer. He was one of the two men who first reached the North Pole. It was a big victory. The year was 1909. One explorer, Robert Peary, became famous. He was given many honors. But Henson, a black man, did not become well known until 1944. In that year he was given a medal for his **outstanding** service to the U.S. Today Henson is honored for his great deed.

1. In this paragraph, the word **outstanding** must mean
   - ○ A. outdoor
   - ○ B. really great
   - ○ C. long

Lunchtime

Mrs Hill entered the crowded lunchroom. She went through the line and chose her food. When she paid, Mrs Hill looked around for a place to sit. There were no empty tables. Mrs Hill spotted a table where people were laughing and talking. They seemed to be having a good time."That's a **merry** group,"she thought."I'll join them."

2. In this paragraph, the word **merry** must mean
   - ○ A. jolly
   - ○ B. hungry
   - ○ C. crowded

To parents Go to page 124 and do Activity 8 with your child.

Exercise 11

Read each paragraph. Then fill in the bubble that best completes each sentence.

Air Highways

Big cities have lots of air traffic. So the air space over these cities is divided into airways. These are like highways for planes. Each airway has a number. The airways also have speed limits. How do pilots know where the airways are? Control towers **beam** radio signals to show the airways. Pilots follow the signals just as drivers use road signs.

1. In this paragraph, the word **beam** must mean
   ○ A. send
   ○ B. smile
   ○ C. speed

At the Cabin

The cabin had been closed up all winter. Inside, it was dim and **gloomy**. Spiderwebs hung in the corners. Dust covered the floors. Mia said, "Let's make this place more cheerful." She opened the wooden shutters to let in light. Then she began sweeping and dusting. Soon the cabin would be ready for summer fun.

2. In this paragraph, the word **gloomy** must mean
   ○ A. dark
   ○ B. clean
   ○ C. cheery

To parents Go to page 124 and do Activity 8 with your child.

Date: _____

Exercise 12

Read each paragraph. Then fill in the bubble that best completes each sentence.

London Bobbies

To the people of London, England, a bobby is a **familiar** sight. A bobby is a police officer. Why are these workers called bobbies? They are named for Sir Robert (Bobby) Peel. He formed the police force in London in 1829.
At that time a lot of people in the city were breaking the law. Today bobbies still make sure the laws are followed in London.

1. In this paragraph, the word **familiar** must mean
   ○ A. well-known
   ○ B. in a family
   ○ C. strange

Where's Owen?

Emma looked up and down the street. There was no sign of Owen. He was so **seldom** late. Where could he be? Emma looked at her watch. For Owen to be 15 minutes late was really unusual. Then, suddenly, Owen appeared around the corner. His leg was in a cast. No wonder it took him so long to get to their meeting place!

2. In this paragraph, the word **seldom** must mean
   ○ A. rarely
   ○ B. often
   ○ C. misplaced

To parents   Go to page 124 and do Activity 8 with your child.

Exercise 13

Read each paragraph. Then fill in the bubble that best completes each sentence.

Cats and Dogs

Animals have different ways to protect themselves. Suppose a strange dog **threatens** a cat. What does the cat do? It stretches its legs and arches its back. It fluffs its fur and turns so its side faces the dog. All this makes the cat look much bigger. In case the dog doesn't get the idea, the cat also hisses!

1. In this paragraph, the word **threatens** must mean
   ○ A. causes a feeling of joy
   ○ B. wants to make friends with
   ○ C. shows signs of hurting

Hide and Seek

At Cole's party, the guests played a game of hide-and-seek. It was Cole's turn to hide. He planned to **crouch** behind a large flowerpot on the porch. But when he got there, his dog, Rags, was already sleeping behind the pot. There was no time to find another place. Quickly, Cole bent down next to his dog. Rags began to bark, and the guests soon found Cole.

2. In this paragraph, the word **crouch** must mean
   ○ A. crumble
   ○ B. stoop
   ○ C. sleep

To parents Go to page 124 and do Activity 8 with your child.

Exercise 14

Read each paragraph. Then fill in the bubble that best completes each sentence.

Volcanoes

An active volcano is quite a sight. Very hot rock boils miles below the top of the volcano. The boiling rock gives off gases. Over time these gases rise to the top of the volcano. Then they blow holes called **vents** in the volcano. Soon great clouds of gas and dust pour from the vents and shoot high in the sky. Hot rock flows out of the vents and down the sides of the volcano.

Aunt Polly's Wash

On Saturday morning Aunt Polly did a big load of wash."It's such a fine day,"she said."I think I'll hang the clothes on the line outside. Then they will **flutter** in the wind and dry."So Aunt Polly hung up her clean clothes. Sure enough, they began to flap. This upset all the birds in the yard, but Aunt Polly was very happy.

1. In this paragraph, the word **vents** must mean
   - ○ A. openings
   - ○ B. winds
   - ○ C. viewings

2. In this paragraph, the word **flutter** must mean
   - ○ A. blow away
   - ○ B. wave fast
   - ○ C. make noise

To parents Go to page 124 and do Activity 8 with your child.

Date: _____

Exercise 15

Read each paragraph. Then fill in the bubble that best completes each sentence.

Good at Business

Madame C. J. Walker had her own business. She sold products for hair care. She also owned beauty shops in many U.S. cities. She set up schools to **train** people to work for her. By 1919 Madame Walker had made a lot of money. She became the first black female millionaire. She gave money to help many black groups. She also helped schools and needy people.

1. In this paragraph, the word **train** must mean
   ○ A. railroad
   ○ B. teach
   ○ C. save

Harry's Show

Harry was telling his family about a show with a juggler. "He wore funny clothes," said Harry. "And he had lots of balls. He could keep them all in the air at the same time." Harry's father was puzzled. How had Harry seen a show? Their TV was broken. "Where did this show **occur**?" Dad asked. "Did you see it at preschool?" Harry shook his head. "It happened in a book!" he said.

2. In this paragraph, the word **occur** must mean
   ○ A. toss around
   ○ B. turn off
   ○ C. take place

To parents Go to page 124 and do Activity 8 with your child.

Exercise 16

Read each paragraph. Then fill in the bubble that best completes each sentence.

The Flamingo

The flamingo is a bird with long legs and a long neck. It takes its food from the lakes where it lives. How does a flamingo **obtain** its food? It lowers its beak upside down into the water. Then it sweeps its head back and forth with its beak open. In this way it catches its favorite food—shrimp.

1. In this paragraph, the word **obtain** must mean
   - ○ A. cook
   - ○ B. chew
   - ○ C. get

Stan's Picture

Stan was drawing a picture. It showed his sister's wedding. She had worn a long white dress. Her husband wore a black tuxedo. Stan put them both in the picture. "You forgot my flowers," said his sister. Stan thought for a moment. "What color were they?" His sister answered, "They were the **hue** of an evening sky."

2. In this paragraph, the word **hue** must mean
   - ○ A. stars
   - ○ B. shape
   - ○ C. color

To parents Go to page 124 and do Activity 8 with your child.

Exercise 17

Read each paragraph. Then fill in the bubble that best completes each sentence.

A Food Story

Long ago there were no freezers or tin cans. People had to think of ways to keep food from going bad. They used different ways to **preserve** food. For example, they dried some fruits, vegetables, and meat. Another way to keep fruits was to make jams from them. People also used salt and water to make food last longer. Some foods such as potatoes could be stored in a cold place.

1. In this paragraph, the word **preserve** must mean
   - ○ A. spoil or destroy
   - ○ B. buy or grow
   - ○ C. keep or save

Sick in Bed

When Terry was sick, she had to stay in bed for a few days. Terry didn't mind. She found lots of ways to **amuse** herself. Her favorite way of spending time was reading. She also did a lot of drawing. In the evenings Terry had fun playing board games with her sister. Once in a while they even watched TV.

2. In this paragraph, the word **amuse** must mean
   - ○ A. entertain
   - ○ B. annoy
   - ○ C. recover

To parents   Go to page 124 and do Activity 8 with your child.

Exercise 18

Read each paragraph. Then fill in the bubble that best completes each sentence.

An Amazing Plant

Can a plant grow through ice? At least one plant can. The blue moonwort grows on the mountains in Switzerland. These mountains are covered with snow and ice during the winter. Early each spring the moonwort soaks up some of the melting snow through its roots. Then its stem starts pushing up. Soon the plant **bores** a hole right through the ice! Then it begins to bloom.

1. In this paragraph, the word **bores** must mean
   ○ A. tires
   ○ B. drills
   ○ C. grows

A Good Cookie

An ant spotted something on the step. It looked like a cookie. Quickly, the ant raced back to its nest to let others know. Soon a line of ants made its way to the cookie. But just then a large foot appeared. It stepped on the cookie and **crushed** it. The ants didn't mind. They waited until the foot moved. Then they picked up the small pieces and carried them to the nest.

2. In this paragraph, the word **crush** must mean
   ○ A. break into pieces
   ○ B. made a noise
   ○ C. carried away

To parents   Go to page 124 and do Activity 8 with your child.

Exercise 19

Read each paragraph. Then fill in the bubble that best completes each sentence.

The Button Story

Why are there buttons on the sleeves of men's jackets? Some say it is because of Frederick the Great. This king led his men in many wars. He liked the troops to look neat. But their sleeves were always dirty. That's because the soldiers wiped the sweat from their faces on their sleeves. Frederick was **outraged** about this. He was so angry he had buttons put on the uniform sleeves of all his men. It's hard to wipe your face on a button.

Ice Cream, Please

Connor worked in an ice cream shop. On a summer day he was very busy. It seemed that everyone loved ice cream then. Each morning Connor checked his supplies. Most people ordered cones. The flavors they chose would **vary** though. Connor was careful to have plenty of each flavor on hand.

1. In this paragraph, the word **outraged** must mean
   ○ A. angry
   ○ B. sweaty
   ○ C. pleased

2. In this paragraph, the word **vary** must mean
   ○ A. plenty
   ○ B. differ
   ○ C. taste

To parents   Go to page 124 and do Activity 8 with your child.

Exercise 20

Read each paragraph. Then fill in the bubble that best completes each sentence.

The Earth and Sun

In 1632 people thought that the sun moved around Earth. They didn't think Earth moved at all. That year Galileo wrote a book. He said that Earth moved around the sun. People were upset. Galileo was told he would be killed unless he said his book was a lie. So Galileo said he had written a lie. But he knew that didn't **alter** the truth. For Earth does move around the sun.

1. In this paragraph, the word **alter** must mean
   - ○ A. worship
   - ○ B. renew
   - ○ C. change

Vito's Test

Vito did **poorly** on a test in school. This upset him because he had worked hard. Vito's dad had an idea. He took Vito to see an eye doctor. Sure enough, Vito needed glasses. Now Vito can see better, and he does well on his tests too.

2. In this paragraph, the word **poorly** must mean
   - ○ A. not well
   - ○ B. just okay
   - ○ C. slowly

To parents Go to page 124 and do Activity 8 with your child.

Inferring

Making inferences is essential in helping a reader better understand what is being communicated in a text. Very often a text does not always include every fact or detail about a topic. Readers often draw upon their own knowledge or experiences to make sense of what is stated in a text. This process of mentally adding on information to aid comprehension is called inferring. The passages and questions in this section will help your child learn to make inferences.

This section will provide opportunities for your child to understand that inferring helps him fill in the information that is unstated and to make sense of a text. This is important as your child encounters a variety of texts and writing styles.

The extension activities provide additional challenges to your child to encourage and develop his understanding of the particular comprehension skill.

Date: _____

Exercise 1

Read each paragraph. Then fill in the bubble that best answers each question.

Trouble in the Pacific

Aloud roar came from an island in the Pacific Ocean. Fiery rock and smoke shot into the sky. People 3,000 miles away heard the noise. Dust hung in the air. Great waves rolled through the sea. They slammed into villages along the coasts of other islands. The damage was huge.

1. Which sentence is most likely true?
   - ○ A. A dragon on the island was angry.
   - ○ B. There was a blizzard on the island.
   - ○ C. A volcano erupted on the island.

In the Display Case

The little boy stood on tiptoe to see inside the display case. He pointed to one of the containers. As the clerk opened the case, the little boy shook his head. He looked some more. He pointed to another container. But, no, that wasn't the one either. Finally, the little boy nodded and pointed to still another container. The smiling clerk began scooping.

2. Which sentence is most likely true?
   - ○ A. The boy is trying to make the clerk angry.
   - ○ B. The boy is choosing an ice cream flavor.
   - ○ C. The store does not have many choices.

To parents   Go to page 124 and do Activity 6 with your child.

Exercise 2

Read each paragraph. Then fill in the bubble that best answers each question.

Be Careful About Customs

You have to be careful about customs. Not everyone follows the same ones. For example, in Japan people remove their shoes before entering a temple. They don't let their socks touch the floor. Instead, they step directly onto a mat called a *tatami*. Many visitors don't know this custom. So sometimes they seem rude.

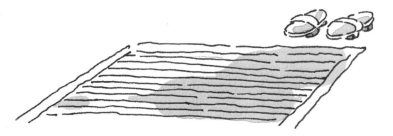

1. Which sentence is most likely true?
   - ○ A. People in Japan go barefoot most of the time.
   - ○ B. Foreigners might not remove shoes at a temple.
   - ○ C. People in Japan think shoes and socks are silly.

Leaving Home

Mr Patel was ready to leave for the day. He kissed his wife and children goodbye. He gave the dog a pat on the head. Then he picked up his briefcase and opened the door. Stepping outside, Mr Patel looked up. He held out his hand. Quickly, he turned around and went back into the house.

2. Which sentence is most likely true?
   - ○ A. Mr Patel wants to say goodbye again.
   - ○ B. Mr Patel forgot to pat the cat.
   - ○ C. Mr Patel went back to get an umbrella.

To parents   Go to page 124 and do Activity 6 with your child.

Exercise 3

Read each paragraph. Then fill in the bubble that best answers each question.

On the River

All year long, powerful tugboats push barges up and down the Hudson River. The barges are loaded with oil, gas, and supplies for factories. In the winter of 2003, the tugboats and barges often got stuck. They had to be rescued by icebreakers. First a breaker would free the frozen boats. Then it would cut a path through the frozen water. Then the river traffic could move again.

1. Which sentence is most likely true?
   - ○ A. The winter of 2003 had low temperatures.
   - ○ B. Tugboats and barges got stuck in the mud.
   - ○ C. Not much happens on the river in winter.

Busy Nan

Nan opened the drawer and took out five forks. She counted out knives and spoons too. Then she got water glasses and plates down from the cabinet. She folded some napkins and found her little brother's bib. Nan even remembered to get out the salt and pepper.

2. Which sentence is most likely true?
   - ○ A. Nan is going to have a tea party.
   - ○ B. Nan works in a large restaurant.
   - ○ C. Nan is setting the table for supper.

To parents   Go to page 124 and do Activity 6 with your child.

Exercise 4

Read each paragraph. Then fill in the bubble that best answers each question.

Numbers

The earliest people didn't have numbers. They probably knew that there were more of some things than others. But people wanted to keep track of what they had. How many sheep did they have? How many spears? At first people made marks on a stick or wall to count things. Later they invented symbols for different amounts. We call these numbers.

1. Which sentence is most likely true?
   ○ A. People invented numbers to keep records.
   ○ B. People had too many things to count.
   ○ C. People had no reason to count things.

Dale's Day

Dale sat at his desk and sharpened a pencil. He stared at the blank pad. No ideas. Sighing, Dale played with his eraser. He looked out the window. He gazed around his room. Maybe a snack would help. Dale ran down to the kitchen for some cookies. Then he called his friend Jack to talk about the assignment. By six o'clock, Dale was getting worried.

2. Which sentence is most likely true?
   ○ A. Jack will do the assignment for Dale.
   ○ B. Dale can't get started writing.
   ○ C. Dale finds it easy to write papers.

To parents Go to page 124 and do Activity 6 with your child.

Exercise 5

Read each paragraph. Then fill in the bubble that best answers each question.

Damage in Pierce City

As the reporters pulled into Pierce City, they couldn't believe all the damage they saw. It seemed to follow a path right through the town. Trees along the road were uprooted. A roof was missing from one house. Two cars were upside down in someone's yard. And in a trailer park, several homes had been blown over.

1. Which sentence is most likely true?
   ○ A. The town was struck by lightning.
   ○ B. The town was really a movie set.
   ○ C. The town was hit by a bad tornado.

Mr Bruno's Ride

Mr Bruno slowed down as he came to the toll. Traffic was heavy, and there were lines of cars in front of him. Slowly, he inched forward. At last he was through the entrance. He drove carefully, staying in his lane and away from the walls. After a mile and a half, he was out in the open again. He was glad to see the sky overhead.

2. Which sentence is most likely true?
   ○ A. Mr Bruno is driving over a bridge.
   ○ B. Mr Bruno is going through a tunnel.
   ○ C. Mr Bruno is at an amusement park.

To parents   Go to page 124 and do Activity 6 with your child.

Exercise 6

Read each paragraph. Then fill in the bubble that best answers each question.

Weaving

In many parts of the world, women make rugs and blankets on hand looms. They use yarn spun from cotton or wool. The yarn is dyed with natural plant colors. The designs that the women weave are age-old. Often the designs and colors have special meaning to a region or group of people.

1. Which sentence is most likely true?
   ○ A. All rugs and blankets are woven by women.
   ○ B. Weaving is a traditional art in many places.
   ○ C. The weaving industry never uses new designs.

Calling Dana

Dana and her parents sat in the first row. Dana was a little nervous, but her parents had big smiles on their faces. Dana clapped politely as the principal called out names. She watched different students go to the stage. Then her name was called! Excitedly, Dana went up on the stage. She could hear her father cheering as the principal held out his hand.

2. Which sentence is most likely true?
   ○ A. Dana is going to become an actress.
   ○ B. Dana has won an award at school.
   ○ C. Dana is in trouble with the principal.

To parents   Go to page 124 and do Activity 6 with your child.

Exercise 7

Read each paragraph. Then fill in the bubble that best answers each question.

Paper Money

Have you ever looked closely at a U.S. five dollar bill? Tiny red and blue fibers are all over the paper. If you hold the bill up to the light, you will see a picture. It is called a watermark. Each bill also has a number that sparkles and changes color. Another number is so small, you need a magnifying glass to read it. All these things make U.S. paper money hard to copy.

1. Which sentence is most likely true?
   - ○ A. No one ever tries to copy U.S. paper money.
   - ○ B. The U.S. does not want anyone to copy its money.
   - ○ C. You need a magnifying glass to use U.S. money.

On the Steps

Jim was sitting on the steps to his house. He was reading a book. He was also waiting for his friends to come over. Suddenly, something tickled Jim's arm. He scratched his arm. A few minutes later it happened again. This time Jim saw that an ant was crawling up his arm. There were ants on the steps, too.

2. Which sentence is most likely true?
   - ○ A. Jim is sitting near an anthill.
   - ○ B. Jim's friends brought ants.
   - ○ C. Jim was reading about ants.

To parents   Go to page 124 and do Activity 6 with your child.

Exercise 8

Read each paragraph. Then fill in the bubble that best answers each question.

A Greek Word

In the Greek language *rhinos* means "nose." Can you see this Greek word in the English word *rhinoceros*? This animal certainly has a big nose! Other English words have *rhinos* in them, too. A rhinovirus might affect your nose. This virus is what people get when they have a cold.

1. Which sentence is most likely true?
   - ○ A. A nose doctor is called a rhinologist.
   - ○ B. A rhinoceros gets a lot of colds.
   - ○ C. The Greek language is full of viruses.

Roger

Roger heard a noise. It was a car coming down the street. Even though he was taking a nap, Roger just had to see who it was. He padded over to the fence. It wasn't a car. It was a truck! Maybe it was the workman he had met yesterday. In a flash, Roger scampered out of his yard.

2. Which sentence is most likely true?
   - ○ A. Roger is a neighborhood dog.
   - ○ B. Roger is a friendly boy.
   - ○ C. Roger is bored with workmen.

To parents Go to page 124 and do Activity 6 with your child.

Exercise 9

Read each paragraph. Then fill in the bubble that best answers each question.

In the Night

Most people do their sleeping during the night. But many wild creatures do not. Mice do much of their roaming at night. It's harder for foxes to hunt them in the dark. When otters live near people, they are more active at night. A dragonfly sheds its skin at night. It takes a few hours for the new adult's wings to grow strong. By morning the dragonfly is ready to fly away.

1. Which sentence is most likely true?
   - ○ A. Otters like to live near people.
   - ○ B. It is safer for some animals at night.
   - ○ C. Wild animals have more fun at night.

What Happened?

One night something furry slipped from the hollow tree. A masked animal crept across the sidewalk. It stopped by a container. With little trouble, the animal got the lid off. Crash! The lid clattered to the ground. Mr Tucker woke up and looked out the window. There was trash on the sidewalk. He could see a striped tail disappear around the corner.

2. Which sentence is most likely true?
   - ○ A. A raccoon got into the garbage.
   - ○ B. Mr Tucker had a bad dream.
   - ○ C. An animal robbed Mr Tucker.

To parents Go to page 124 and do Activity 6 with your child.

Exercise 10

Read each paragraph. Then fill in the bubble that best answers each question.

A Book Story

Thomas Rockwell wrote a book called *How to Eat Fried Worms*. Did he ever eat a worm? Rockwell thought he probably should. He decided that if the book got published, he would eat a worm. Somehow he never found the time. Rockwell did talk to a doctor about worms though. Are they safe to eat? The doctor said worms are good for people.

1. Which sentence is most likely true?
   - ○ A. Rockwell probably didn't want to eat a worm.
   - ○ B. Rockwell hoped the doctor would buy his book.
   - ○ C. Rockwell was sure that readers wouldn't eat worms.

What's the Time?

A faint light came from the East. Slowly, it spread over the town. One by one, the street lamps went out. Traffic noises began to pick up. Runners made their way along paths by the river. The first workers hurried to cars and trains. Students appeared to climb onto waiting buses. People put on glasses to protect their eyes from the rising sun.

2. Which sentence is most likely true?
   - ○ A. It is early morning.
   - ○ B. It is early evening.
   - ○ C. It is late morning.

To parents   Go to page 124 and do Activity 6 with your child.

Exercise 11

Read each paragraph. Then fill in the bubble that best answers each question.

Looking at Laws

Governments make laws when a community needs them. Sometimes laws made in the past seem silly today. For example, it is not lawful to tickle a girl in Norton, Virginia. If you go to Maine, be sure to tie your shoelaces. It is against the law to have them undone. And don't sneeze on trains in West Virginia. You will be breaking the law.

1. Which sentence is most likely true?
   - ○ A. All communities have the same laws.
   - ○ B. Silly laws help people behave well.
   - ○ C. The reasons for laws change over time.

A Question for José

José gazed out the window. He could hear the second graders on the playground. It sounded like they were having fun. José wished he could be with them. But someone was saying his name. Quickly, José looked at the front of the room. His face got red, and he shook his head. No, he hadn't heard the question.

2. Which sentence is most likely true?
   - ○ A. José is on the playground.
   - ○ B. José is studying at home.
   - ○ C. José is in a classroom.

To parents Go to page 124 and do Activity 6 with your child.

Exercise 12

Read each paragraph. Then fill in the bubble that best answers each question.

Frog Features

Did you know that frogs can fly? In Asia some frogs have webbed feet that act like parachutes. South America has poison frogs. One of these can kill 20,000 mice! Frogs in Europe have lived to be almost 40 years old. Frogs in Africa can be as big as footballs. And in North America some frogs freeze during the winter. They thaw out again in the spring!

1. Which sentence is most likely true?
   - ○ A. Frogs are alike no matter where they live.
   - ○ B. Frogs can be found on many continents.
   - ○ C. Frogs can fly from continent to continent.

Ali's List

Ali made a list of the things he needed. He started with his water bottle. Then he added gloves. Next came shorts, shoes, and a helmet. "Don't forget your fanny pack," said his sister. So Ali wrote that on the list. He also added lunch. His mother had promised to make him a sandwich for the trip.

2. Which sentence is most likely true?
   - ○ A. Ali is going to a football game.
   - ○ B. Ali is going on a hiking trip.
   - ○ C. Ali is going on a biking trip.

To parents   Go to page 124 and do Activity 6 with your child.

Exercise 13

Read each paragraph. Then fill in the bubble that best answers each question.

Long Ago News

Long ago there was no TV. No one had a radio. There were no computers. And there were very few newspapers. How did people get news? One way was from a town crier. This person walked through the streets and called out the news. If something special happened, the town crier beat a drum or rang a bell. People would run to hear the news.

1. Which sentence is most likely true?
   - ○ A. There were few ways to get news long ago.
   - ○ B. Most news in the past appeared in print.
   - ○ C. In the past, people weren't interested in news.

Helping Lena

Lena woke up from a long nap. She tried to sit up, but it was too much trouble. Her mother came into the room. She had a tray with some juice on it. She patted the pillows and smoothed the sheets. Then she helped Lena sit up. "Try to drink this," said Lena's mom. "It's good for you."

2. Which sentence is most likely true?
   - ○ A. Lena is a patient in a hospital.
   - ○ B. Lena is sick in bed at home.
   - ○ C. Lena had a bad nightmare.

To parents   Go to page 124 and do Activity 6 with your child.

Exercise 14

Read each paragraph. Then fill in the bubble that best answers each question.

The First Sailors

The first sailors were amazed at some of the creatures they saw. They didn't know what these strange animals were. They thought that whales were monsters. They thought that lizards were dragons. As a result, mapmakers began to put monsters and dragons on the edges of maps. They believed that these fearful creatures came from places no one had yet explored.

1. Which sentence is most likely true?
   - ○ A. The first sailors had seen whales and lizards in books.
   - ○ B. People were afraid of things they didn't know about.
   - ○ C. Early mapmakers could identify all places on the globe.

John Decides

John turned the pages slowly. He looked at all the pictures. Sometimes he read the text below them. John noted the prices of things too. Finally, he made up his mind. He went to the phone and dialed. Then John explained what he wanted.

2. Which sentence is most likely true?
   - ○ A. John is reading a library book.
   - ○ B. John is looking at a photo album.
   - ○ C. John is ordering from a catalog.

To parents   Go to page 124 and do Activity 6 with your child.

Exercise 15

Read each paragraph. Then fill in the bubble that best answers each question.

In Minnesota

Minnesota is in the northern part of the U.S. This state has more than 10,000 lakes. Most of them freeze by December. People sometimes drive on the lakes then. During the winter the city of St. Paul has a big carnival. One event is an ice-carving contest. In Minneapolis, people use skywalks to go from building to building. That way they don't have to go outside in winter.

1. Which sentence is most likely true?
   - ○ A. Minnesota has very cold winters.
   - ○ B. Minnesota has no sidewalks or roads.
   - ○ C. People carve ice in Minnesota's lakes.

Ziggy and Dad

As they entered the park, Ziggy could see the horses. She asked her dad to hurry. She wanted to ride on her favorite horse. After her dad bought tickets, Ziggy ran to her horse and took the reins. Her dad helped her up. Then he climbed on the horse next to Ziggy. Soon the music began. Ziggy smiled and enjoyed her ride.

2. Which sentence is most likely true?
   - ○ A. Ziggy is visiting a horse farm.
   - ○ B. Ziggy is on a merry-go-round.
   - ○ C. Ziggy is taking riding lessons.

To parents   Go to page 124 and do Activity 6 with your child.

Exercise 16

Read each paragraph. Then fill in the bubble that best answers each question.

The Giant Cactus

A giant cactus grows in the desert. By the time the cactus is 150 years old, it is full of holes. In one hole lives a bat. Another hole is home to some insects. Birds lay eggs and raise families in the cactus, too. Even some pack rats find a place to live in the cactus. When one animal leaves the cactus, others move in.

1. Which sentence is most likely true?
   ○ A. The animals are harmful to the cactus.
   ○ B. The cactus provides a safe home for animals.
   ○ C. Only flying animals live in the cactus.

The Drink Machine

It was hot, and Mr Santos was thirsty. He went down to the basement of the building. He found the drink machine. But Mr Santos didn't have the right change. He went upstairs and got it. Then he went back to the machine. In went his quarters. Nothing happened. Mr Santos pressed the coin return. Nothing. He banged on the machine. Nothing. He even kicked the machine. Still nothing.

2. Which sentence is most likely true?
   ○ A. Mr Santos is losing his temper.
   ○ B. Mr Santos is no longer thirsty.
   ○ C. Mr Santos will fix the machine.

To parents Go to page 124 and do Activity 6 with your child.

Date: _____

Exercise 17

Read each paragraph. Then fill in the bubble that best answers each question.

New Cars

It was the year 1903. Cars were still a pretty new product. They didn't look the way they do today. For example, when it rained, drivers couldn't see through the windshield. Instead, they had to lean their heads out the window. That gave Mary Anderson an idea. Her invention solved the problem and kept drivers dry.

1. Which sentence is most likely true?
   - ○ A. Mary Anderson invented special car umbrellas.
   - ○ B. Mary Anderson invented convertible cars.
   - ○ C. Mary Anderson invented windshield wipers.

Kate's Meal

Kate was having dinner in a restaurant. She decided to order something different. When her meal came, Kate took a big bite. It was good. But then Kate's eyes opened wide. She began to cough. Her face turned red. Tears rolled down her cheeks. Quickly, Kate grabbed a glass of water and drank it down. She asked for another.

2. Which sentence is most likely true?
   - ○ A. Kate ate something hot and spicy.
   - ○ B. Kate is suddenly very sad.
   - ○ C. Kate ordered a very sweet dessert.

To parents Go to page 124 and do Activity 6 with your child.

Exercise 18

Read each paragraph. Then fill in the bubble that best answers each question.

Home in a Castle

Long ago, most kings lived in castles. Castles were often built on steep hills. Their walls were high and very thick. Some castles had secret tunnels. People used the tunnels to escape if enemies came. Many castles also had moats around them. These were ditches filled with water. To enter a castle, visitors had to go over a bridge that was let down on chains. They then went through an entrance with a spiked gate.

1. Which sentence is most likely true?

   ○ A. It was easy to get inside a castle.

   ○ B. Castles were built for protection.

   ○ C. Everyone was welcome at a castle.

You've Got Mail!

Suki got an e-mail from her friend. The message made Suki happy. She went to talk to her mother. Then she checked the calendar. When she finished her homework, Suki wrote back to her friend. The answer was "Yes!"

2. Which sentence is most likely true?

   ○ A. The friend sent greetings to Suki's mother.

   ○ B. The friend asked about some homework.

   ○ C. Suki made a date to see her friend.

To parents   Go to page 124 and do Activity 6 with your child.

Drawing Conclusions

Being able to draw accurate conclusions from the information provided in a text helps is essential to help readers derive meaning from language with layers of implied meaning. The skill of drawing conclusions is related to that of making inferences, particularly when a text does not always state every bit of information explicitly. Readers often have to piece together the clues that the writer provides and then draw the best conclusions they can to understand the text. The passages and questions in this section will help your child learn to make inferences.

This section will provide opportunities for your child to understand that drawing conclusions helps him fill to use evidence in the text to come to make sense of text and to read between the lines. This is important as your child encounters a variety of texts and writing styles.

The extension activities provide additional challenges to your child to encourage and develop his understanding of the particular comprehension skill.

Exercise 1

Read the paragraph. Then fill in the bubble that best completes each sentence.

Ponds form when rainwater accumulates in hollows in the ground. In the past, people believed that ponds caused sickness and brought bad luck because wizards lived there. Many ponds were dried out and built over to increase the size of fields. However, we now realize that ponds are vital for the survival of all sorts of animals and plants. They are constant sources of water for many birds and insects, as well as covers for frogs. When faced with danger, frogs and other insects often dive down into the ponds. In addition, pond plants also provide oxygen and food to many animals.

1. From this paragraph, you can conclude that
   ○ A. water snakes live in ponds.
   ○ B. there is a constant supply of fresh water in the pond.
   ○ C. ponds are used by many animals.
   ○ D. the water in the pond becomes ice in winter.

2. From the paragraph, you cannot tell
   ○ A. how deep a pond can be.
   ○ B. a pond supplies oxygen to the pond animals.
   ○ C. how ponds are formed.
   ○ D. why people disliked ponds in the past.

To parents   Go to page 124 and do Activity 7 with your child.

Exercise 2

Read the paragraph. Then fill in the bubble that best completes each sentence.

Many riding centers these days offer special programs for children with disabilities or emotional needs. Horses are intelligent and loving animals. Getting acquainted and being around them help children with special needs to be calm and relaxed. Initially, children learn to groom horses. Helping to groom a horse allows them to feel useful as they are usually the ones being cared for. When they are comfortable enough with their horses, they start riding. Riding helps children gain assurance, balance and concentration. Learning to stay on and control the horses gives children self-confidence – a useful trait wherever they go.

1. From this paragraph, you can conclude that
   - ○ A. horse riding is an expensive sport.
   - ○ B. horse riding is a fantastic sport for children with disabilities or emotional needs.
   - ○ C. children with special needs need special gear for riding.
   - ○ D. children with special needs love horses.

2. From the paragraph, you cannot tell
   - ○ A. if children usually ride bare-back.
   - ○ B. if riding programs for children with special needs are common.
   - ○ C. if it is important for children with special needs to be calm.
   - ○ D. if children are first taught to groom horses.

To parents Go to page 124 and do Activity 7 with your child.

Exercise 3

Read the paragraph. Then fill in the bubble that best completes each sentence.

Sharks are at the mercy of mankind. Over one hundred million sharks are killed yearly and many populations are facing extinction. With advanced navigational electronics, shark fishing has become common and relatively easy. Sharks are sought after for many reasons such as fear, food and sports. However, majority of the sharks perish due to the greed of mankind. Many shark products have high commercial value. The skin is used for leather and its liver oil for cosmetics, medicines and skin care products. The most valuable part of a shark, however, is its fins. They are used to make a delicacy — shark's fin soup.

1. From this paragraph, you can conclude that
   - ○ A. sharks are dangerous.
   - ○ B. shark's fin is the secret to a beautiful complexion.
   - ○ C. shark's teeth and jaws are used to make ornaments.
   - ○ D. more people are fishing for sharks now.

2. From the paragraph, you cannot tell
   - ○ A. the reasons sharks are sought after.
   - ○ B. why shark fishing is easier now.
   - ○ C. that sharks are left to die an agonizing death in the water after their fins are sliced off.
   - ○ D. that a huge number of sharks are killed each year.

To parents   Go to page 124 and do Activity 7 with your child.

Exercise 4

Read the paragraph. Then fill in the bubble that best completes each sentence.

We all forget things once in a while, but Alzheimer's Disease, a condition which affects some older people, is different. It permanently affects the brain, and makes it hard for patients to remember even basic things. Patients may have difficulty remembering family members or even who he or she is. Researchers believe that factors such as high blood pressure, high cholesterol, Down Syndrome, head injuries, when combined with hereditary factors, can increase the likelihood of having Alzheimer's Disease. However, medication can help to slow down the effects of the disease. Exercise, a healthy diet, and taking steps to keep your mind active may delay the onset of Alzheimer's Disease too.

1. From this paragraph, you can conclude that
    ○ A. Alzheimer's Disease affects the patient's ability to care for himself.
    ○ B. doctors take detailed pictures of the brain.
    ○ C. all head injuries will lead to Alzheimer's Disease.
    ○ D. Alzheimer's Disease can be cured.

2. From the paragraph, you cannot tell
    ○ A. that playing chess may delay the onset of Alzheimer's Disease.
    ○ B. why Alzheimer's Disease is more likely to affect older people.
    ○ C. that everyone forgets things occasionally.
    ○ D. that people with Alzheimer's Disease may forget their own names.

To parents   Go to page 124 and do Activity 7 with your child.

Exercise 5

Read the paragraph. Then fill in the bubble that best completes each sentence.

Do you know why we blush? There are thousands of blood vessels under our skin. Blood makes fair skin look pink but is less visible with darker skin. When we feel emotions like anger or embarrassment, our bodies release a substance called adrenaline to help us react. Adrenaline in our bloodstream enlarges the blood vessels. This means more blood flows beneath the skin, making it red. People with dark skin blush too, but it is less obvious. Besides our emotional state, high temperatures, alcohol and certain illnesses and medications can also cause us to blush.

1. From this paragraph, you can conclude that
   ○ A. blushing is good for health.
   ○ B. girls blush more often than boys.
   ○ C. blushing helps to release heat in your bodies.
   ○ D. blushing cannot be controlled.

2. From the paragraph, you cannot tell
   ○ A. that blushing is a result of our enlarged blood vessels.
   ○ B. that the fear of blushing causes more embarrassment and blushing.
   ○ C. that people with dark skins blush too.
   ○ D. that adrenaline is a substance released by our bodies.

To parents Go to page 124 and do Activity 7 with your child.

Exercise 6

Read the paragraph. Then fill in the bubble that best completes each sentence.

Martin Luther King Jr. led in the civil rights movement in the United States. He helped convince many white Americans to support the cause of civil rights. King encouraged the use of nonviolent marches, demonstrations, and boycotts to protest against discrimination. He and other black leaders organized the 1963 March on Washington, where he delivered his famous "I Have a Dream" speech. The speech and the march created the political momentum that resulted in the Civil Rights Act of 1964. The Act prohibited racial separation in public places and discrimination in education and employment. King was awarded the 1964 Nobel Prize for his work.

1. From this paragraph, you can conclude that
   - ○ A. King has four children.
   - ○ B. King was a peace loving man.
   - ○ C. King often dreamed at night.
   - ○ D. King was ordained as a Baptist minister.

2. From the paragraph, you cannot tell
   - ○ A. why the blacks were discriminated.
   - ○ B. that King was an inspiring speaker and a respected leader.
   - ○ C. that the Civil Rights Act of 1964 prohibited segregation and discrimination based on race.
   - ○ D. that some white Americans also supported the cause of civil rights.

To parents Go to page 124 and do Activity 7 with your child.

Exercise 7

Read the paragraph. Then fill in the bubble that best completes each sentence.

The story of the cacao tree began around 400 B.C. in the tropical rainforests of Central and South America. The pods of this tree contain seeds that became the main ingredient for making chocolate. Besides using cacao seeds as money, the ancient Mayans also mixed grounded cacao seeds with various seasonings to make a frothy drink. Later, the Spanish brought these seeds back to Spain, where new recipes were created. The drink's popularity spread throughout Europe. Since then, new technologies and innovations have transformed the plain cacao seeds into various mouth-watering products. Till now, chocolate still remains popular.

1. From this paragraph, you can conclude that
   - ○ A. cacao trees are cash crops in South America.
   - ○ B. cacao seeds were made into chocolate milk by the Mayans.
   - ○ C. chocolate means warm liquid.
   - ○ D. chocolate has been popular for a long period of time.

2. From the paragraph, you cannot tell
   - ○ A. the Spanish helped make chocolate popular.
   - ○ B. Spain planted cacao trees in its overseas colonies.
   - ○ C. the Mayans used cacao seeds as money.
   - ○ D. cacao trees were first found in the rainforests of South and Central America.

To parents   Go to page 124 and do Activity 7 with your child.

Exercise 8

Read the paragraph. Then fill in the bubble that best completes each sentence.

The wolf spider is a unique member of the arachnid family. Unlike most spiders, they are not found in webs. Instead, they burrow holes in the ground. Even though the wolf spider is fierce, the female is considered to be a very protective mother. She produces an egg sac that contains over 100 eggs. She attaches the sac to her body and carries it with her wherever she goes. When the eggs hatch, the spiderlings crawl out of the eggs. They crawl onto their mother's abdomen and hold on to the hair there. They stay protected by their mother for a week before leaving her.

1. From this paragraph, you can conclude that
   - ○ A. wolf spiders do not spin webs.
   - ○ B. wolf spiders eat small insects.
   - ○ C. a wolf spider is a large spider.
   - ○ D. the wolf spider uses leaves to cushion its burrow.

2. From the paragraph, you cannot tell
   - ○ A. how wolf spiders catch their prey.
   - ○ B. if wolf spiders are protective mothers.
   - ○ C. how wolf spiders protect its spiderlings.
   - ○ D. that wolf spiders are unlike most spiders.

To parents Go to page 124 and do Activity 7 with your child.

Exercise 9

Read the paragraph. Then fill in the bubble that best completes each sentence.

Abraham Lincoln spent his childhood in toil and hardship. His family was poor and everyone had to work on the farm. After laboring all day, Lincoln would read by the light of the burning fire until he fell asleep. He had little chance to get an education. However, he learned to read books such as *Aesop's Fables*, *The Pilgrim's Progress*, and the Bible. Once he borrowed the book, *Life of Washington* from a neighbor. He kept it in a crevice in the wall for safety. One night it rained heavily and the book was thoroughly soaked. His neighbor made him work three days in exchange for the wet book. That was the first book Lincoln owned.

1. From this paragraph, you can conclude that
   ○ A. Lincoln was the youngest in his family.
   ○ B. Lincoln was successful because he was a determined person.
   ○ C. Lincoln's neighbour was a kind person.
   ○ D. Lincoln had a great passion for reading.

2. From the paragraph, you cannot tell
   ○ A. the title of the first book owned by Lincoln.
   ○ B. if young Lincoln had to work on the farm.
   ○ C. if Lincoln had gone to school briefly.
   ○ D. when Lincoln read.

To parents   Go to page 124 and do Activity 7 with your child.

Date: _____

Exercise 10

Read the paragraph. Then fill in the bubble that best completes each sentence.

Coral reefs are very important to mankind. They are homes to many species of reef fish and molluscs. They provide shelter and protection, as well as a place for these sea creatures to have babies. Corals also help to control the amount of carbon dioxide in the ocean. Without them, the amount of carbon dioxide in the ocean would rise drastically. This would, in turn, affect all living things on earth. Lastly, corals also provide a barrier between the ocean and the shore. They slow down the water before it reaches the shore, thus protecting the coasts from strong currents and waves.

1. From this paragraph, you can conclude that
   ○ A. corals prefer salt water.
   ○ B. coral reefs are made by man.
   ○ C. corals take in carbon dioxide.
   ○ D. fish and molluscs like coral reefs because they are beautiful.

2. From the paragraph, you cannot tell
   ○ A. that reefs provide shelter and protection for fish.
   ○ B. where coral reefs are commonly found.
   ○ C. why reefs are also called barrier reefs.
   ○ D. that coral reefs are important to mankind.

To parents Go to page 124 and do Activity 7 with your child.

Exercise 11

Read the paragraph. Then fill in the bubble that best completes each sentence.

Many people claim that crystals help in spiritual awakening, physical healing, and promoting harmonious relationships. Crystals are often used in meditation and laid on the body when a person is resting or placed in bathing waters. It is believed that clear and aquamarine crystals are healers, red and orange crystals give energy, and blue-violet crystals produce calming effects. However, there is no scientific evidence that crystals work. Crystal therapy practitioners believe that crystals focus energy using a person's positive thoughts and then conduct them to his physical body, thus helping to stimulate healing.

1. From this paragraph, you can conclude that
   ○ A. people use crystals to communicate with spirits.
   ○ B. crystals are expensive.
   ○ C. the effectiveness of crystals is questionable.
   ○ D. crystals are made into different jewelry.

2. From the paragraph, you cannot tell
   ○ A. that crystals aid in healing.
   ○ B. if a person who needs physical healing will wear a clear crystal.
   ○ C. if people believe crystals help in spiritual awakening.
   ○ D. that in crystal therapy, positive thinking is important.

To parents   Go to page 124 and do Activity 7 with your child.

Exercise 12

Read the paragraph. Then fill in the bubble that best completes each sentence.

Bats are the only mammals that can fly. They cannot survive in extremely cold weather, thus some fly to places with warmer climate during winter. Others hibernate in caves or tunnels where the temperature remains constant and they will not be disturbed. When hibernating, bats hang upside down. Many people think that bats are blind. On the contrary, bats can see as well as man. At night or in dark places, however, bats use echoes to locate things. As they fly, they make high-pitched sounds that cannot be heard by humans. The echoes they get back will provide them with information about what lies ahead of them.

1. From this paragraph, you can conclude that
   ○ A. a bat's ears are more important than their eyes at night.
   ○ B. a bat looks like a winged rat.
   ○ C. a bat's vision is better than a man's.
   ○ D. bats have wings and feathers.

2. From the paragraph, you cannot tell
   ○ A. that man cannot hear the high-pitched sounds made by bats.
   ○ B. why bats hang upside down.
   ○ C. that bats dislike extremely cold weather.
   ○ D. that bats are warm-blooded animals.

To parents Go to page 124 and do Activity 7 with your child.

Exercise 13

Read the paragraph. Then fill in the bubble that best completes each sentence.

Many people assume that yawning is a sign of boredom. However, recent research has shown that yawning actually perks one up. We tend to yawn before an important event – we yawn before an interview, pilots yawn before take-off and even animals yawn before a fight. Some findings suggest that yawning prepares our brain for a change. A baby in the womb may yawn as it shifts its position. Yawning is highly contagious. If we spot someone with his mouth open, we are likely to follow. However, we are more likely to yawn if the person yawning is someone we like or are close to.

1. From this paragraph, you can conclude that
   - ○ A. adults yawn more often than children.
   - ○ B. children begin to copy other people's yawn at the age of four or five.
   - ○ C. yawning occurs to both people and animals.
   - ○ D. boys are more likely to yawn than girls.

2. From the paragraph, you cannot tell
   - ○ A. that we yawn before important events.
   - ○ B. why we yawn before bed time.
   - ○ C. that yawning helps us to get ready for change.
   - ○ D. we tend to yawn when we spot someone yawning.

To parents   Go to page 124 and do Activity 7 with your child.

Exercise 14

Read the paragraph. Then fill in the bubble that best completes each sentence.

Reduce, reuse and recycle – the 3Rs to keep our earth healthy. These words seem to hang on everyone's lips these days. We see recycling bins and second-hand item stores all around town. Why is there a sudden need for the 3Rs? Our natural resources are depleting at a drastic rate in recent years. More and more trees are cut down for timber, paper and for the development of towns and villages. Deforestation causes wild animals to lose their natural habitats and affects the balance of our atmosphere. If we do not protect our forests now, we may have to bear with the irreversible impact of our actions in the near future.

1. From this paragraph, you can conclude that
   - ○ A. many people think recycling is a waste of time.
   - ○ B. our natural resources can be replenished easily.
   - ○ C. global warming helps make the world a better place to live in.
   - ○ D. forests are essential to the survival of mankind.

2. From the paragraph, you cannot tell
   - ○ A. if animals lose their habitats as a result of deforestation.
   - ○ B. the rate at which forests are being cut down.
   - ○ C. that people clear forests to make space for the development of towns.
   - ○ D. if more people are aware of the 3Rs these days.

To parents Go to page 124 and do Activity 7 with your child.

Exercise 15

Read the paragraph. Then fill in the bubble that best completes each sentence.

Auckland, New Zealand's largest city, has a population of 1.3 million. Like many busy cities, it is characterized by high-rise buildings, rush-hour traffic and bustling shopping malls. However, what makes Auckland different from a typical city is its charming village feel. The air is cool and refreshing and the streets are relatively safe. People are generally friendly and helpful. Visitors to Auckland can experience a whole range of outdoor activities such as bungee jumping, jet boating or mountain climbing. Alternatively, they may simply choose to enjoy the breathtaking scenery of majestic mountains and cascading waterfalls.

1. From this paragraph, you can conclude that
   ○ A. Auckland's main income comes from tourism.
   ○ B. visitors to Auckland spend quite a bit of their time outdoors.
   ○ C. people in Auckland love nature.
   ○ D. Auckland has a good public transportation system.

2. From the paragraph, you cannot tell
   ○ A. which is the best time of the year to visit Auckland.
   ○ B. people in Auckland are peace loving.
   ○ C. people who enjoy outdoor adventures are likely to enjoy visiting Auckland.
   ○ D. Auckland has waterfalls and mountains.

To parents   Go to page 124 and do Activity 7 with your child.

Exercise 16

Read the paragraph. Then fill in the bubble that best completes each sentence.

The dishevelled sloth bears are found in the forests of
South Asia where termites and ants abound, providing
them with a ready supply of food. Sloth bears have unique
features that help their feeding lifestyle. For example,
their long, curved claws enable them to rip open hard
termite mounds. They also have a long, white muzzle with
protruding lips. The sloth bear uses its lips like a vacuum,
making rapid, loud noises as it sucks insects from their
nests. The sucking noises made by the sloth bear can be
heard up to 90 meters away. To adapt to the tropical heat,
the sloth bear has no underfur. Its long shaggy coat helps
to prevent insect bites.

1. From this paragraph, you can conclude that
   - ○ A. sloth bears are nocturnal animals.
   - ○ B. sloth bears are endangered.
   - ○ C. sloth bears lead solitary lives.
   - ○ D. sloth bears adapt well to their environment.

2. From the paragraph, you cannot tell
   - ○ A. sloth bears eat termites and ants.
   - ○ B. sloth bears carry their young on their backs.
   - ○ C. sloth bears belong to the bear family.
   - ○ D. why sloth bears have long shaggy coats.

To parents Go to page 124 and do Activity 7 with your child.

Date: _____

Exercise 17

Read the paragraph. Then fill in the bubble that best completes each sentence.

Many families wash their clothes at public laundromats. Often, parents must take their children along with the dirty clothes and pockets of coins when they do the laundry. To give the children something worthwhile to do while their parents fold clean clothes, one laundry chain started a Wash and Learn program. The program operates during after-school hours and in the evenings. At special tables set up in the laundry, students can listen to stories, read books by themselves, and get help with their homework. Several teachers are on hand to help.

1. From this paragraph, you can conclude that
   - ○ A. some students do their homework at school.
   - ○ B. students get grades at the Wash and Learn program.
   - ○ C. the program is helpful to both parents and children.
   - ○ D. the program shows children how to wash clothes.

2. From the paragraph, you cannot tell
   - ○ A. what the name of the program is.
   - ○ B. what the children do in the program.
   - ○ C. when the program operates.
   - ○ D. how much laundry the parents do.

To parents   Go to page 124 and do Activity 7 with your child.

Exercise 18

Read the paragraph. Then fill in the bubble that best completes each sentence.

When a word has been shortened, it is called a clip. For example, a *ref* is a short form of the word *referee*. Over time, many words in English have been clipped. Do you know the original word for a *mike*? It's *microphone*. Something that is a *curio* was once a *curiosity*. You probably enjoy visiting the *zoo*, but at one time people visited a *zoological garden*. Perhaps you go to and from school on a *bus*. Students of the past traveled on an *omnibus*. School words such as *math* and *exams* are simplified versions of *mathematics* and *examinations*.

1. From this paragraph, you can conclude that
   ○ A. it is harder to learn clipped words.
   ○ B. riding on an omnibus was not safe.
   ○ C. clips are easier to pronounce and spell.
   ○ D. people don't like to use short words.

2. From the paragraph, you cannot tell
   ○ A. the number of clips in the English language.
   ○ B. what the shortened word for *zoological garden* is.
   ○ C. what the word *mike* came from.
   ○ D. how to spell the word *curiosity*.

To parents Go to page 124 and do Activity 7 with your child.

Summarizing

Summarizing helps a reader identify the important points in a text and make sense of what is being communicated in a text. Very often, writers provide many details as examples of what they mean but these examples are not necessary in conveying the essential message in the passage. That is where summarizing is important. Readers are required to condense the information that they read and to restate the ideas in the text using their own words or phrases. By summarizing, readers learn to identify the main ideas and differentiate the essential information from the details. The passages and questions in this section will help your child learn to summarize a passage.

This section will provide opportunities for your child to read a text closely to pick out the central ideas in a text and understand which are the details supporting the text. He is then required to use the information he has sifted out to form a summary. This is important as your child encounters a variety of texts and various forms of communication.

The extension activities provide additional challenges to your child to encourage and develop his understanding of the particular comprehension skill.

Exercise 1

Read the paragraph. Then answer the questions.

Sailors have always needed lighthouses to warn them of dangerous conditions. The first tower that was built for such a purpose was at the entrance to Port Alexandria, a long-ago capital of ancient Egypt. The tower, called Pharos, was very large. It was so impressive a structure that it was known as one of the seven wonders of the ancient world. Fire beacons burning on the tower helped ships navigate through the treacherous waters approaching the city.

1. What was the name of the first lighthouse?

   _____

2. Where was it located?

   _____

3. Why was it a wonder?

   _____

4. The title that best summarizes this paragraph is

   ○ A. Burning Fire Beacons in the Night

   ○ B. Pharos, the First Lighthouse Tower

   ○ C. Helping Ships Navigate Tricky Waters

   ○ D. A Look at Ancient Egypt

   Use your answers to help you write a short summary of the paragraph.

   _____

   _____

   _____

To parents Go to pages 123 and 124 and do Activity 1 or 9 with your child.

106

Exercise 2

Read the paragraph. Then answer the questions.

Everyone knows that thousands of athletes compete in the Olympic Games and that hundreds of thousands of visitors attend. But did you know that about 60,000 more people work to make the Olympics run smoothly? Some of these workers are paid, but thousands of others are volunteers. All of them have to be trained for their job. These workers do everything from sweeping up litter to escorting competitors to selling tickets to announcing winners.

1. Who makes the Olympics run smoothly?

   _____

2. How do these people know what to do?

   _____

3. What kinds of jobs do these people do?

   _____

   _____

4. The title that best summarizes this paragraph is

   ○ A. How Athletes Compete at the Games

   ○ B. Working as a Ticket Seller

   ○ C. Tips for Visitors to the Olympics

   ○ D. Workers Behind the Olympics

Use your answers to help you write a short summary of the paragraph.

_____

_____

_____

To parents Go to pages 123 and 124 and do Activity 1 or 9 with your child.

107

Exercise 3

Read the paragraph. Then answer the questions.

What does it take to be a survivor? Gary Paulsen knows. This well-known writer had a difficult boyhood and left home at age 14. He worked with a carnival, on a farm, on a ranch, and as a truck driver. He's also been a teacher, editor, and singer. Today, Paulsen receives more than 400 letters a day from readers who identify with the struggles of the main character in his award-winning books, *Hatchet, Brian's Winter,* and *The River.* When he's not writing, Paulsen enjoys sailing and adventure.

1. Who is Gary Paulsen?

   _____

2. What has his life been like?

   _____

   _____

3. What does he do when he's not writing?

   _____

4. The title that best summarizes this paragraph is

   ○ A. Reading Gary Paulsen's Books

   ○ B. Why Paulsen Left Home at Age 14

   ○ C. Paulsen: Survivor in Life and Literature

   ○ D. Getting to Know Book Characters

Use your answers to help you write a short summary of the paragraph.

_____

_____

_____

To parents   Go to pages 123 and 124 and do Activity 1 or 9 with your child.

108

Exercise 4

Read the paragraph. Then answer the questions.

The explorer Marco Polo left his home in Italy in 1271. After many years of traveling, his party reached the summer palace of Kublai Khan in what is now China. Polo remained at the court for 17 years. He marveled at things not yet seen in Europe. For example, common people bathed daily. Roads and bridges were paved. People used paper money as currency. They also burned coal as a fuel. When Polo finally returned to Europe, it took a while before people believed the stories he told or the book he wrote about his travels.

1. Where did Marco Polo go?

   _____

2. What amazed him about China?

   _____

   _____

3. Why didn't people believe him on his return?

   _____

4. The title that best summarizes this paragraph is

   ○ A. What Marco Polo Was Like
   ○ B. Meeting Kublai Khan
   ○ C. A Wanderer From Italy
   ○ D. The Travels of Marco Polo

   Use your answers to help you write a short summary of the paragraph.

   _____

   _____

   _____

To parents   Go to pages 123 and 124 and do Activity 1 or 9 with your child.

109

Exercise 5

Read the paragraph. Then answer the questions.

At one time, people thought that blowing dust was the way to clean. Then in the 1870s Hubert Booth, an engineer, tried placing a handkerchief between his mouth and a couch and sucking in. The film of dirt on the other side of the hanky suggested that suctioning in dirt was the way to clean. Booth designed fans that sucked dust into pillow cases. He even sold some to the Queen of England. About 30 years later, the Hoover Company came out with an upright suctioning machine on rollers. The rest is vacuum cleaner history.

1. Who was Hubert Booth?

   _____

2. What did his experiment suggest?

   _____

3. How did the Hoover Company improve on this concept?

   _____

   _____

4. The title that best summarizes this paragraph is

   ○ A. The First Vacuum Cleaners
   ○ B. How the Queen Cleaned
   ○ C. Blowing in the Dust
   ○ D. What Hoover Did

   Use your answers to help you write a short summary of the paragraph.

   _____

   _____

   _____

To parents   Go to pages 123 and 124 and do Activity 1 or 9 with your child.

110

Exercise 6

Read the paragraph. Then answer the questions.

You know that spiders spin silk, but do you know what spiders do with their silk? Mother spiders keep the eggs they lay in silk sacs. Spiders also use their silk to make webs or homes. Many spiders have hideouts in places such as window corners or under sills. They line the entrances to these places with silk. Spiders also use silk threads to drop straight to the ground when enemies appear. And, of course, spiders can spin silken traps and nets to catch their dinner.

1. How do spiders make homes?
   _____

2. How do spiders stay safe?
   _____

3. How do spiders catch food?
   _____

4. The title that best summarizes this paragraph is

   ○ A. How Spiders Find Food
   ○ B. A Spider's Use of Silk
   ○ C. Spinning Silken Clothes
   ○ D. Outwitting Spider Enemies

   Use your answers to help you write a short summary of the paragraph.

   _____

   _____

   _____

To parents Go to pages 123 and 124 and do Activity 1 or 9 with your child.

111

Exercise 7

Read the paragraph. Then answer the questions.

Earthquakes cause buildings to fall and injure or kill people. So engineers and architects are trying to make buildings safer. Skyscrapers are built so that they sway but don't fall when earthquakes strike. Some buildings are put on rollers while others have steel beams anchored into the ground. Builders also use stronger and more flexible materials. A new idea is to put heavy weights in buildings so that if they move one way, the weight moves the other way to help keep the building from toppling.

1. How do earthquakes harm people?

   _____

2. How do engineers try to make buildings safer?

   _____

3. What new idea might help?

   _____

   _____

4. The title that best summarizes this paragraph is

   ○ A. How Earthquakes Harm Us
   ○ B. Why Skyscrapers Sway
   ○ C. Limiting Earthquake Damage
   ○ D. Engineers and Architects at Work

Use your answers to help you write a short summary of the paragraph.

_____

_____

_____

To parents   Go to pages 123 and 124 and do Activity 1 or 9 with your child.

Exercise 8

Read the paragraph. Then answer the questions.

In the early years of the United States, land travel was difficult. Roads were no more than dirt paths that became rutted and muddy with rain. Finally, Congress decided to build a National Road. Work began at Cumberland, Maryland, in 1811. After seven years, the road stretched west to the Ohio River at Wheeling in what is now West Virginia. It wasn't until 1852 that the road reached its end at Vandalia, Illinois. In its time, thousands of settlers used the road to travel westward.

1. Why was a National Road built?

   _____

2. Where and when did it begin and end?

   _____

   _____

3. Who used the road?

   _____

4. The title that best summarizes this paragraph is

   ○ A. Traveling in America
   ○ B. Building the National Road
   ○ C. Why Dirt Roads Don't Work
   ○ D. Who Used the National Road

   Use your answers to help you write a short summary of the paragraph.

   _____

   _____

   _____

To parents Go to pages 123 and 124 and do Activity 1 or 9 with your child.

Exercise 9

Read the paragraph. Then answer the questions.

Turtles have been around for more than 200 million years. Scientists think they are the most ancient of all reptiles. Turtles live in many places on land and in water. Like all reptiles, they are cold-blooded. Turtles that live where winters are cold usually hibernate. Turtles eat insects, fish and frogs. They also munch on plants, including fruit and flowers. The largest turtle is the leatherback, which can weigh more than 2,000 pounds!

1. How long have turtles existed?
   _____

2. Where do turtles live?
   _____

3. What do they eat?
   _____

   _____

4. The title that best summarizes this paragraph is

   ○ A. Interesting Facts About Turtles
   ○ B. Very Ancient Reptiles
   ○ C. The Large Leatherback
   ○ D. Places Where Turtles Live

Use your answers to help you write a short summary of the paragraph.

_____

_____

_____

To parents   Go to pages 123 and 124 and do Activity 1 or 9 with your child.

114

Exercise 10

Read the paragraph. Then answer the questions.

Scorpions are known as the living fossils because they have not changed much in form in the last 400 million years. Like humans, they change their habits to adapt to the environment. Scorpions are so versatile that they can be found almost everywhere on earth; from mountainous areas to the shores, from deserts to rainforests. They have a low metabolic rate as they do not do much. Most species spend majority of their time close to their burrows. Scorpions are survivors because they are not choosy about food. They can consume a large amount of food but excrete little. Some species can go without food for a year; some can even live indefinitely without water.

1. Where can we find scorpions?

   _____

2. What do they eat?

   _____

3. What is special about them?

   _____

   _____

4. The title that best summarizes this paragraph is

   ○ A. The Living Fossils
   ○ B. Survival of the Fittest
   ○ C. On Hunger Strike
   ○ D. How to Go Without Food

Use your answers to help you write a short summary of the paragraph.

_____

_____

_____

To parents   Go to pages 123 and 124 and do Activity 1 or 9 with your child.

Exercise 11

Read the paragraph. Then answer the questions.

Pyramids are the stone tombs of the pharaohs and one of the world's greatest historical mysteries. They come in different shapes and sizes and have stood for thousands of years. The ancient Egyptians believed that if the pharaoh's body was mummified after death, the pharaoh would have eternal life. Pyramids were thus built to protect the mummified Pharaoh's body and his belongings. Most of the pyramids can be found on the west bank of the Nile River because it was believed that the sun 'died' on the western horizon every night. The most famous pyramid was the 'Great Pyramid', built for the pharaoh Khufu.

1. What are pyramids?

   _____

2. Where were they built?

   _____

3. Why did the ancient Egyptians build pyramids?

   _____

4. The title that best summarizes this paragraph is

   ○ A. The Great Pyramid
   ○ B. Khufu, The Great Ruler
   ○ C. Pyramids
   ○ D. Pharaohs

Use your answers to help you write a short summary of the paragraph.

_____

_____

_____

To parents Go to pages 123 and 124 and do Activity 1 or 9 with your child.

Exercise 12

Read the paragraph. Then answer the questions.

What is a volcano? It is a mountain that opens downward to a pool of magma below the surface of the earth. As pressure in the magma builds up, it forces its way up narrow cracks in the earth's crust. Once the magma erupts through the earth's surface, it is called lava. Volcanic eruptions can have devastating effects. Eruptions can result in lava flows, hot ash flows, mudslides, avalanches and floods. There are more than 1500 active volcanoes in the world, of which 80 or more are under the oceans. Over half of the world's volcanoes arise in a belt called the 'Ring of Fire' around the Pacific Ocean.

1. What is a volcano?

   _____

2. When does it erupt?

   _____

3. What can eruptions result in?

   _____

   _____

4. The title that best summarizes this paragraph is

   ○ A. Effects of Volcanic Eruptions

   ○ B. Volcanoes and Effects of Volcanic Eruptions

   ○ C. What is a Volcano?

   ○ D. A Natural Disaster

Use your answers to help you write a short summary of the paragraph.

_____

_____

_____

To parents Go to pages 123 and 124 and do Activity 1 or 9 with your child.

Exercise 13

Read the paragraph. Then answer the questions.

Mother Teresa was born in Macedonia in 1910. She was the recipient of the 1979 Nobel Peace Prize. She received the calling "to be God's Love in action to the poorest of the poor" on her journey to Darjeeling. She then started a new order of Sisters and they began their mission to help the poor in Calcutta. They were given a part of an abandoned temple of Kali. They then brought the sick and dying on the city's streets to Kalighat Home for the Dying, founded by Mother Teresa. Mother Teresa also steered the expansion of the Missionaries of Charity, first throughout India and then in other countries. She passed away in 1997.

1. Who was Mother Teresa?

   _____

2. Why didn't Mother Teresa go to Darjeeling?

   _____

3. What did Mother Teresa do?

   _____

   _____

4. The title that best summarizes this paragraph is

   ○ A. Mother Teresa's Life
   ○ B. Life in Calcutta
   ○ C. Mother Teresa's Deeds
   ○ D. God's Calling

Use your answers to help you write a short summary of the paragraph.

_____

_____

_____

To parents Go to pages 123 and 124 and do Activity 1 or 9 with your child.

Exercise 14

Read the paragraph. Then answer the questions.

Birds sleep in their normal habitats. Birds that you see in trees during the day also sleep there during the night. Birds are light sleepers and they must be constantly aware of their surroundings. They sleep higher and closer to the end of the branch. This gives them more cover, and more warning when they feel the vibrations of a predator approaching. Amazingly, birds do not fall off when they sleep on the branch due to a special muscle in their legs. When they sleep, their "knees" bend backwards, tightening the muscle that locks their legs and feet in position.

1. Where do birds sleep?

   _____

2. Why do birds sleep higher and closer to the end of the branches?

   _____

3. Why do birds not fall off when they sleep on the branch?

   _____

   _____

4. The title that best summarizes this paragraph is

   ○ A. Sleeping Habits of Birds
   ○ B. Why Birds Sleep Without Falling
   ○ C. Light Sleepers
   ○ D. Eating Habits of Birds Falling

Use your answers to help you write a short summary of the paragraph.

_____

_____

_____

To parents Go to pages 123 and 124 and do Activity 1 or 9 with your child.

Exercise 15

Read the paragraph. Then answer the questions.

Claude Monet was born in Paris in 1840. As a teenager, he developed a reputation as a caricature artist. Later, Claude met landscape painter Eugene-Louis Boudin. Eugene introduced Claude to landscape painting. The ocean inspired him and he liked the way light reflected off objects and water. Claude believed that landscape was an impression and an instantaneous one. His work "Impression, Sunrise" had an unpolished look. The brush strokes were lively and spontaneous, capturing the mood of the moment. This painting style was unusual and different from his predecessors', thus earning him the title of an "Impressionist".

1. Who was Claude Monet?

   _____

2. What kind of painting was Claude introduced to?

   _____

3. How were Claude's paintings different from his predecessors'?

   _____

4. The title that best summarizes this paragraph is

   ○ A. Claude Monet's Life
   ○ B. Caricature Artist
   ○ C. The Rise of Impressionism
   ○ D. Claude Monet, the Impressionist

   Use your answers to help you write a short summary of the paragraph.

   _____

   _____

   _____

To parents   Go to pages 123 and 124 and do Activity 1 or 9 with your child.

Exercise 16

Read the paragraph. Then answer the questions.

Leather is made of cured animal skin. Early man wrapped uncured animal skin around him to keep out the cold. Later, he learned that hanging the uncured skins in the smoke near a fire prevented them from decaying. Eventually, he discovered that soaking them in a substance derived from plants called tannin not only prevented them from rotting, but also softened the hides and changed their colours. The softened hides were easier to shape and the hair could be removed easily. This process to preserve animal skin is known as tanning. Skins of calves, crocodiles, deer, snakes and ostriches are popular choices for leather.

1. What is leather?

   _____

2. What is tanning?

   _____

3. Why were animal skins cured?

   _____

4. The title that best summarizes this paragraph is

   ○ A. Different Kinds of Leather
   ○ B. The Making of Leather
   ○ C. Intelligent Early Man
   ○ D. Keeping Warm

   Use your answers to help you write a short summary of the paragraph.

   _____

   _____

   _____

To parents   Go to pages 123 and 124 and do Activity 1 or 9 with your child.

121

Exercise 17

Read the paragraph. Then answer the questions.

Consumers often spend a few puzzled moments looking at egg cartons in supermarkets. That's because there are six official egg sizes. The sizes are determined by weight. A jumbo, the largest-size egg, weights 30 ounces while a peewee egg, the smallest size, weighs only 15 ounces. In between are extra-large, large, medium, and small eggs. Most markets only stock the four largest sizes; small and peewee eggs are usually sold to bakers and companies in the food processing business.

1. How many official egg sizes are there?

   _____

2. How are egg sizes determined?

   _____

3. What are the different egg sizes?

   _____

4. The title that best summarizes this paragraph is

   ○ A. Egg Cartons
   ○ B. The Weight of Eggs
   ○ C. Eggs and Their Sizes
   ○ D. The Life of an Egg

   Use your answers to help you write a short summary of the paragraph.

   _____

   _____

   _____

To parents   Go to pages 123 and 124 and do Activity 1 or 9 with your child.

Extension Activities

Activity 1: What's the Title?

Skill: Identifying main ideas / Summarizing

Prepare 3 newspaper or magazine articles. Cut away the titles and read each article with your child. Ask him to think of a suitable title for each article. Then have your child match the original titles to each article. Extend this activity to include the skill of summarizing by asking your child to pick out a few important points from each article. Then get him to put the points together to form a summary of the article.

Activity 2: A Main Idea Card

Skill: Identifying main idea and details

Have your child make a card about someone he knows well. Write a main idea about that person on the front of the card. For example, Grandpa is good at fixing things. Then ask your child to illustrate his idea using pictures. Next, have your child write details to support his main point, for example, Grandpa fixed my bicycle when it broke down.

Activity 3: What am I?

Skill: Making Predictions

Prepare 3 to 4 photographs of different events. Have your child predict what might have happened after showing him each photograph. Encourage him to come up with predictions based on evidences from the photographs, prior knowledge, and his own personal experiences.

Activity 4: Detective Time

Skill: Identifying Fact and Opinion

Select two different types of texts for your child – one that predominantly has facts (entries in reference books or newspaper articles) and one that predominantly has opinions (editorials or advertisements). From each type of article, get your child to identify clues that suggest whether a particular sentence is factual or based on opinion.

Activity 5: Alike and Different

Skill: Comparing and Contrasting

Ask your child to list points about two things / people / places and categorize the points. Then get him to highlight the similarities in one color and the differences in another color. Get your child to write a short paragraph about the two items. He can use the texts in this book as examples.

Activity 6: Piecing Things Together

Skill: Inferring

Find a picture book or prepare a series of pictures that might tell a story. Now show your child the pictures. Have your child infer the story based on the pictures. Remember to ask him at each point why he thought the story would progress in a certain way. Your child should use clues in the pictures as well as his own knowledge to make inferences.

Activity 7: Make a Guess

Skill: Drawing Conclusions

Find a descriptive paragraph about a character. The character could be doing an activity or experiencing an emotion. Be sure that the emotion or activity is not actually named in the text. Then get your child to read the text and ask him to guess the activity or emotion. Remember to ask your child why he drew those conclusions.

Activity 8: What's That Word?

Skill: Using Context Clues

Select a few paragraphs. Replace a familiar word with one that is unfamiliar to your child. Then ask your child to read the whole paragraph to try and determine the meaning of the unfamiliar word. Ask him to identify the clues in the text.

Activity 9: Paint a Flower

Skill: Summarizing

Read a story with your child. Make a flower with 5 petals and a long stem. Write the title of the story on the first petal. Draw the character of the story on the second petal, the setting of the story on the third petal, the problem of the story of a fourth petal and the resolution of the story on the fifth petal. Then have your child verbally summarize the story using the pictures he has drawn.

Answer key

Page 7

I . C   2. B

Page 8

I . C   2. B

Page 9

I . C   2. A

Page 10

I . A   2. D

Page 11

I . C   2. B

Page 12

I . B   2. B

Page 13

I . C   2. C

Page 14

I . A   2. D

Page 16

I . C   2. B

Page 17

I . B   2. B

Page 18

I . B   2. B

Page 19

I . A   2. C

Page 20

I . A   2. C

Page 21

I . C   2. A

Page 22

I . B   2. A

Page 23

I . B   2. A

Page 25

1. A. Opinion   B. Fact   C. Fact
2. He was born in Russia in 1920.
3. *Fantastic Voyage* was definitely his best book.

Page 26

1. A. Opinion   B. Opinion   C. Fact
2. Snowflakes form when water vapor condenses into crystals.   3. Each snowflake is a work of art.

Page 27

1. A. Opinion   B. Fact   C. Fact
2. In the tomb were 6,000 life-sized soldiers made from terra-cotta. 3. I think this is bizarre.

Page 28

1. A. Opinion   B. Opinion   C. Fact
2. Japan has regular radio and television programs about poetry.   3. I wish they were in other nations.

Page 29

1. A. Opinion   B. Fact   C. Opinion
2. One reason given is that comic strips are reduced when printed in newspapers.
3. I find this really annoying.

Page 30

1. A. Fact   B. Opinion   C. Fact
2. The mountains were formed about 60 million years ago.   3. They must have been brave.

Page 31

1. A. Opinion   B. Opinion   C. Fact
2. This city hosts an annual celebration called Mud Day in Hines Park.   3. That's a lot of mud!

Page 32

1. A. Fact   B. Fact   C. Opinion

2. When finished, however, it will be 563 feet tall and 641 feet long.   3. The head is magnificent.

Page 33

1. A. Opinion   B. Fact   C. Fact
2. During World War II, 350 of them worked as code talkers.   3. You have to be brilliant to break a code.

Page 34

1. A. Opinion   B. Fact   C. Opinion
2. Scientists in China have been sending seeds into space.   3. They're probably not safe!

Page 36

1. A   2. B   3. Boys went to school but girls did not.

Page 37

1. A   2. A   3. Both kinds are plant eaters.

Page 38

1. C   2. B   3. Both kinds of camels groan when they have to rise with heavy loads.

Page 39

1. C   2. C   3. Philadelphia is in the eastern part of the state while Pittsburgh is in the western part.

Page 40

1. A   2. C   3. Paul Bunyan was a lumberman while Pecos Bill was a tall-tale cowboy.

Page 41

1. A   2. B   3. Girder bridges rest on piers while big steel cables support suspension bridges.

Page 42

1. C   2. B   3. Girls could not go to school.

Page 43

1. B   2. A   3. McDonald's mascot is a smiling clown in bright, yellow costume, while KFC's mascot is the cartoonised version of its original creator.

Page 44

1. C   2. A   3. Cameras in the past had to be pre-loaded with film.

Page 45

1. C   2. B   3. Hurricanes are often accompanied by heavy rain and flooding.

Page 47

1. C   2. C

Page 48

1. C   2. A

Page 49

1. A   2. A

Page 50

1. B   2. C

Page 51

1. C   2. B

Page 52

1. C   2. A

Page 53

1. B   2. B

Page 54

1. A   2. C

Page 55

1. C   2. C

Page 56

1. B   2. A

Page 57

1. A   2. A

Page 58

1. A   2. A

Page 59

1. C   2. B

Page 60

1. A   2. B

Page 61

1. B   2. C

Page 62

1. C   2. C

Page 63

1. C   2. A

Page 64

1. B   2. A

Page 65

1. A   2. B

Page 66

1. C   2. A

Page 68

1. C   2. B

Page 69

1. B   2. C

Page 70

1. A   2. C

Page 71

1. A   2. B

Page 72

1. C   2. B

Page 73

1. B   2. B

Page 74

1. B   2. A

Page 75

1. A   2. A

Page 76

1. B   2. A

Page 77

1. A   2. A

Page 78

1. C   2. C

Page 79

1. B   2. C

Page 80

1. A   2. B

Page 81

1. B   2. C

Page 82

1. A   2. B

Page 83

1. B   2. A

Page 84

1. C   2. A

Page 85

1. B   2. C

Page 87

1. C   2. A

Page 88

1. B   2. A

Page 89

1. D   2. C

Page 90

1. A   2. B

Page 91

1. D   2. B

Page 92

1. B   2. A

Page 93

1. B   2. B

Page 94

1. A   2. A

Page 95

1. D   2. C

Page 96

1. C   2. B

Page 97

1. C   2. A

Page 98

1. A   2. B

Page 99

1. C   2. B

Page 100

1. D   2. B

Page 101

1. B   2. A

Page 102

1. D   2. B

Page 103

1. C   2. D

Page 104

1. C   2. A

Page 106

1. Pharos   2. Port Alexandria   3. It had an impressive structure.   4. B

Page 107

1. Workers   2. They are trained   3. Sweep up litter, sell tickets, escort competitors, announce winners 4. D

Page 108

1. A writer   2. Difficult   3. Sailing and adventure   4. C

Page 109

1. China   2. It amazed him that common people bathed daily, roads and bridges were paved, paper money was used and coal was burned as fuel.   3. The things he saw were not yet seen in Europe.   4. D

Page 110

1. An engineer   2. Suctioning in dirt was the way to clean   3. It produced an upright suctioning machine on rollers 4. A

Page 111

1. By spinning silk   2. They hide in window corners or under sills. 3. By spinning silken traps   4. B

Page 112

1. They cause buildings to fall.   2. They use stronger and more flexible material   3. Putting heavy weights in buildings   4. C

Page 113

1. To facilitate land travel in the United States   2. It began in Cumberland, Maryland, in 1811 and ended in Vandalia, Illinois, in 1852.   3. Settlers   4. B

Page 114

1. More than 200 million years 2. On land and in water 3. Insects, fish, frogs and plants 4. A

Page 115

1. Almost everywhere on earth   2. Anything 3. They are very versatile   4. A

Page 116

1. Stone tombs of the pharaohs 2. On the bank of the Nile River 3. To protect the mummified Pharoah's body and his belongings   4. C

Page 117

1. A mountain that opens downward to a pool of magma below the surface of the earth.   2. When pressure in the magma builds up and forces its way up narrow cracks in the earth's crust.   3. Lava flows, hot ash flows, mudslides, avalanches and floods   4. B

Page 118

1. She was the recipient of the 1979 Nobel Peace Prize. 2. She received a calling to start a mission to help the poor in Calcutta.   3. She founded the Kalighat Home for the Dying.   4. A

Page 119

1. In trees   2. It gives them more cover and more warning of predators approaching.   3. Their knees bend and tighten the muscle that locks their leg and feet in position.   4. A

Page 120

1. An artist   2. Landscape   3. They were lively and spontaneous, capturing the mood of the moment. 4. A

Page 121

1. Cured animal skin.   2. A process to preserve animal skin.   3. To prevent them from decaying 4. B

Page 122

1. Six   2. By weight   3. Jumbo, extra-large, large, medium, small and peewee   4. C